W9-BIN-783

r.gr
5/09

The Death of TalkRadio?

INTRODUCTION BY REP. MIKE PENCE, R- IND.

The Death of Talk Radio?

Cliff Kincaid
&
Lynn Woolley

Accuracy in Media

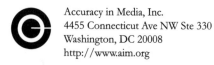

Accuracy in Media, Inc.
4455 Connecticut Ave NW Ste 330
Washington, DC 20008
http://www.aim.org

Copyright © 2007 Accuracy in Media

All rights reserved, including the right of reproduction in whole or part in any form. Quoted passages will be attributed in accordance with the Fair Use provisions of U.S. copyright laws. Material herein may be quoted only if proper attribution is given.

Accuracy in Media logo and colophon are registered trademarks of Accuracy in Media, Inc., a non-profit 501(c)(3) corporation.

For information about special discounts for bulk purchases, please contact Accuracy in Media at 1-800-787-4567 or info@aim.org.

Design by Manuel Gomez

Printed in the United States of America

10 9 8 7 6 5 4 3 2 1

First Edition

Publisher's Cataloging-In-Publication Data
(Prepared by The Donohue Group, Inc.)

Kincaid, Cliff.
    The death of talk radio? / Cliff Kincaid & Lynn Woolley ; introduction by Mike Pence. -- 1st ed.

    p. ; cm.

    ISBN-13: 978-0-9676658-7-0
    ISBN-10: 0-9676658-7-6

1. Fairness doctrine (Broadcasting) 2. Radio in politics--United States. 3. Radio talk shows--United States--Political aspects. 4. Radio broadcasting--United States--Political aspects. 5. Right and left (Political science) I. Woolley, Lynn, 1949- II. Pence, Mike. III. Title.

HE8689.7.F34 K56 2007
384.54/43   2007939753

To three great talk show hosts: Ed Busch, Barry Farber and Rush Limbaugh.

Lynn Woolley

For Reed Irvine, founder of Accuracy in Media, and his legacy of accuracy and truth in media.

Cliff Kincaid

CONTENTS

INTRODUCTION

BY REP. MIKE PENCE, R- IND.

The American people love a fair fight and so do I, especially where the issues of the day are debated. In a free market, fairness should be determined based upon equal opportunity, not equal results. Some voices are calling for Congress to enforce their idea of "fairness" on our broadcast airwaves. But our nation should proceed with caution whenever some would achieve their "fairness" by limiting the freedom of others.

Beginning in 1949, the Federal Communications Commission and its precursor developed and enforced the so-called Fairness Doctrine. The Fairness Doctrine required broadcasters to present controversial issues in a fair and balanced manner. But there's nothing fair about the Fairness Doctrine. To avoid administrative costs and hours of paperwork and legal fees, broadcasters opted to offer noncontroversial programming. As a result, talk radio, as we know it today, simply did not exist.

Recognizing the chilling effect that the regulation was having on broadcast freedom, the FCC began to overturn its own ruling on the

Fairness Doctrine in 1985. Following that change in policy and President Reagan's veto of attempts to reinstate it, the results have been dramatic.

The lifting of the Fairness Doctrine opened the public airwaves to a free and vigorous discussion of controversial issues that never existed before its repeal. When Rush Limbaugh began his legendary career, there were 125 talk radio stations in America. Today there are 2,000. While Limbaugh, Sean Hannity and other conservative giants dominate the national syndicated market, many moderate and liberal programs succeed admirably at the local level.

Since the demise of the Fairness Doctrine, talk radio has emerged as a dynamic forum for public debate and an asset to the nation.

Unfortunately, in the name of fairness, there has been much talk recently about the need to level the playing field of radio broadcasting by restoring this archaic regulation of radio and television.

The liberal Center for American Progress published a report entitled, "The Structural Imbalance of American Talk Radio" in June of this year. The foundation, which is run by former Clinton Chief of Staff John Podesta, lamented the "massive imbalance" of the radio airwaves in a report calling for a whole range of new content and ownership regulations. While stopping short of calling for a return of the Fairness Doctrine, the Podesta group advocated new regulations that could have even a greater chilling effect on broadcast freedom.

Some of the nation's most powerful elected officials have said that Congress should bring back this outright regulation of the American political debate. Sen. Dianne Feinstein told Fox News Sunday that she was "looking at" bringing back the Fairness Doctrine and Sen. John Kerry and Sen. Dick Durbin have both expressly advocated its return. The top Democratic leadership of the House opposed a modest effort to pass a one-year moratorium on the Fairness Doctrine this summer. Leading voices in the Democratic Party, in and out of public office, are advocating a return to regulation of the broadcast airwaves of America.

According to recent polling, some Americans have a willing ear. In a recent Rasmussen national poll, 41 percent of those surveyed would require radio and TV stations to offer equal amounts of conservative and liberal commentary and only 41 percent would oppose. Liberals are even more supportive of the Fairness Doctrine than conservatives. They support the measure by a 51 to 33 percent margin while conservatives are opposed by a 48 to 40 percent margin. To those who cherish our broadcast freedom, we clearly have some work to do educating the nation.

Bringing back the Fairness Doctrine would amount to government control over political views expressed on the public airwaves. It is dangerous to suggest the government should be in the business of rationing free speech. During my years in radio and television, I developed a great respect for a free and independent press. Since being in Congress, I have been the recipient of praise and criticism from broadcast media, but it has not changed my fundamental belief that a free and independent press must be vigorously defended by those who love liberty and limited government.

Congress must take action to ensure that this archaic remnant of a bygone era of American radio does not return. It was in this spirit that I introduced the Broadcaster Freedom Act in July of this year.

The Broadcaster Freedom Act will prohibit the Federal Communications Commission from prescribing rules, regulations, or policies that will reinstate the requirement that broadcasters present opposing viewpoints in controversial issues of public importance. The Broadcaster Freedom Act will prevent the FCC or any future president from reinstating the Fairness Doctrine.

Thanks to the strong support of Minority Leader John Boehner, Minority Whip Roy Blunt and radio station owner and broadcaster

Rep. Greg Walden (R-OR), the Broadcaster Freedom Act is now co-sponsored by all of the 202 Republican members of the House. This unanimous Republican support for any measure is rare and demonstrates the GOP's strong opposition to broadcast censorship. Only one Democrat, Rep. John Yarmuth (D-KY) has cosponsored the bill but my hope is that many Democrats will follow. More than 100 Democrats supported our one-year moratorium of the Fairness Doctrine this summer (see appendix).

In the Senate, Sen. Norm Coleman, Sen. Jim DeMint, Sen. John Thune and Sen. Jim Inhofe have been leading the charge for broadcast freedom. Sen. Coleman introduced the Broadcaster Freedom Act as an amendment twice, only to be filibustered on the Senate floor. These Republican leaders, and Minority Leader Mitch McConnell, should be commended for their strong stand against censorship of the airwaves.

The time has come to do away with the Fairness Doctrine once and for all. The Broadcaster Freedom Act would ensure that no future president could re-regulate the airwaves of America without an act of Congress and it should be sent to the President's desk.

John F. Kennedy stated, "We are not afraid to entrust the American people with unpleasant facts, foreign ideas, alien philosophies, and competitive values. For a nation that is afraid to let its people judge the truth and falsehood in an open market is a nation that is afraid of its people."

America is a nation of freedom and strong opinion. Our government must not be afraid to entrust our good people with all the facts and opinions necessary to make choices as an informed electorate. Let's pass the Broadcaster Freedom Act and consign the Fairness Doctrine to the ash heap of broadcast history where it belongs.

THE BROADCASTER FREEDOM ACT (H.R. 2905 IN THE HOUSE AND S. 1748 IN THE SENATE)

A BILL

To prevent the Federal Communications Commission from re-promulgating the fairness doctrine.

Be it enacted by the Senate and House of Representatives of the United States of America in Congress assembled,

SECTION 1. SHORT TITLE.

This Act may be cited as the "Broadcaster Freedom Act of 2007".

SEC. 2. FAIRNESS DOCTRINE PROHIBITED.

Title III of the Communications Act of 1934 is amended by inserting after section 303 (47 U.S.C. 303) the following new section:

SEC. 303A. LIMITATION ON GENERAL POWERS: FAIRNESS DOCTRINE.

"Notwithstanding section 303 or any other provision of

this Act or any other Act authorizing the Commission to prescribe rules, regulations, policies, doctrines, standards, or other requirements, the Commission shall not have the authority to prescribe any rule, regulation, policy, doctrine, standard, or other requirement that has the purpose or effect of reinstating or repromulgating (in whole or in part) the requirement that broadcasters present opposing viewpoints on controversial issues of public importance, commonly referred to as the 'Fairness Doctrine', as repealed in General Fairness Doctrine Obligations of Broadcast Licensees, 50 Fed. Reg. 35418 (1985).".

I

THE WAY THINGS
USED TO BE

BY LYNN WOOLLEY

"
e who want to fight against fairness."
–U.S. Rep. Louise Slaughter (D-NY)
to Bill Moyers, Dec. 17, 2004

I stand before another assembly of talk radio fans, entertaining them as best I can with stories of the "good old days" when FM was still an alternative medium and rock and roll deejays still ruled on AM. I explain that talk shows were often programmed late at night or on Sunday morning for the purpose of fulfilling a station's "public affairs commitment."

I go on to relate my first experience in talk radio—as news anchor on "The Ed Busch Show" on WFAA in Dallas in 1973. I tell my audience about Ed's guests—the first being a gentleman named Tom Valentine who was an expert on the pyramids of Egypt. I go down the list of Ed's most popular subjects: Author Brad Steiger of *Mysteries of Time and Space;* Joey the Mafia hit man who called from a mobile telephone so the call couldn't be traced; Dr. Peter Beter whose theory was that Nelson Rockefeller was going to become president and later dictator of the United States; and Erich von Daniken whose book *Chariots of the Gods* postulated that ancient astronauts were responsible for such

1

mysteries as Stonehenge and the giant statues of Easter Island.

BUT WHAT ABOUT THE VITAL ISSUES OF THE DAY?

Someone asks, "What about politics? Did the show ever cover political issues like Rush does today?"

"No," I say. I explain that, while politics wasn't taboo, it was considered stuffy and boring. When radio dabbled into political issues, it was usually on Sunday morning, it was canned (recorded), and it seemed purposefully dull.

Ed's show was anything but.

He delighted in bringing on controversial figures such as the atheist Madalyn Murray O'Hair, and once paired her with Dr. W. A. Criswell of Dallas' huge First Baptist Church in a debate that was picked up by a statewide radio network, and videotaped to run on the Dallas ABC affiliate.

I tell my audience about Ed's interviews with a larger-than-life lady by the name of Elizabeth Carmichael who had two automobiles in the post-development stage: the "Dale" and the "Revette." Liz and her investors' cash went missing, and when found by the police, "she" turned out to be one "Jerry Dean Michael." CAR-michael, indeed!

I remember for my audience those evenings that Ed would ring up the Motion Picture Country House, a California living center for retired actors, and get into lengthy discussions of the old Three Stooges shorts with the two then-surviving members of the comedy troupe, Larry Fine and Moe Howard. I smile at the remembrance of these old talk shows, and liken them somewhat to today's Art Bell and George Noory.

As to the question of why Ed Busch rarely delved into the politics of the day, I explain that Ed's show was simply intended as entertainment in a day when no one thought a political show could be anything but dull. Ed obviously enjoyed the subject matter, as did his late-night audience. I tell the crowd that I suspect that Ed did an occasional episode that could be counted by station management as "public affairs," thereby fulfilling one of the requirements of then-current Federal Communications Commission (FCC) regulations.

GOVERNMENT KNOWS BEST

Then, I mention the Fairness Doctrine.

The audience is stunned. They can't believe that speech was regulated by government rules and regs—and during such a recent time. "How can that be?" they want to know. "What about the First Amendment?"

I attempt to explain the old argument that the broadcast spectrum is "owned by the people," but my audience isn't buying it. They are incredulous that government once interfered with their right to tune in to open political discussions on radio or TV.

"If you don't like a radio show, change the channel," someone yells out.

"Agreed," I say. But back in the "good old days," we were all used to the regulation of free speech. We had never heard or even heard of Rush or Sean, and virtually no one had any idea what he was missing.

"Thank goodness we aren't under that kind of restriction today," someone offers.

I smile, and after a pause for effect, I tell the crowd that it's entirely possible to return to those days when the government could yank a company's license to broadcast if it deemed a political show to be not "balanced" under the rules.

I explain that mainstream broadcasts were protected because of the exemption for legitimate news programming. Of course, that meant, that under the guise of news, ABC, CBS and NBC were free to be as biased as they pleased. But if a radio show stopped talking about UFO's and started commenting, Rush-like, about President Nixon, the War in Vietnam, or the emerging welfare state—better call in someone with an opposing viewpoint.

What do I mean when I say that we could return to those days?

I tell my audience that the Left doesn't like to be challenged. After decades of near-complete control of all major media outlets, the New Media revolution caught them by surprise. They can't believe that they actually have major on-air opposition. Sure, they still have the three networks and big newspapers like The New York Times and The Washington Post, but network viewership is rapidly declining and newspapers face unprecedented competition from the internet, talk radio and cable television.

In short, I say, there's an abundance of opinion on the air, in print and in cyberspace—and a lot of it conflicts with conventional liberal wisdom. What's a Leftist to do?

If you're Al Gore, and you're a global warming alarmist, you say that the science is decided and that there should be no more discussion. If you're U.S. Rep. Louise Slaughter, D-NY, you crusade to bring back the Fairness Doctrine in the name of, well, fairness. Who could possibly want to "fight against fairness" she asks. And so, Rep. Slaughter's MEDIA ACT seeks to do just that.

I make sure everyone in the room understands fully that the Left has tried repeatedly to bring back this most-favored regulation only to see prior bills vetoed (or stopped due to threat of veto) during the Reagan and Bush-41 administrations. The crowd is astonished, not realizing that the efforts to regulate on-air speech had come so close to reinstatement.

So far, to no avail, I explain.

Liberal Logic and Long-Form Radio

And so the Left tried a new tack: a liberal-leaning radio network called Air America that failed miserably.

Someone asks why.

"I can only present you with a theory," I answer. My guess is that liberalism only makes sense in short sound bites. When a liberal talk show host has three hours a day to explain kooky ideas such as nationalizing the healthcare system, his arguments collapse under their own weight. But when conservative ideas and values are stripped of emotion and analyzed with truth and logic, they stand up to the scrutiny.

And so, I tell the fans, if liberal values go nowhere under the microscope of long-form radio, the next-best thing to do is find a way to get the opposing viewpoint that DOES make sense off the air. It's like the poker player who sees that he can't win the game, so he kicks the table over and sends the cards reeling.

In the field of ideas, the Left is trying to kick over the table.

"I'll be happy to stay and sign some books," I say in closing. And while I'm putting my John Henry to a few volumes that I brought along to sell, the conversation continues.

"Is this a serious threat?"

"Are we going to lose Rush Limbaugh?"

I tell them, no, we're not going to lose Rush as long as we're vigilant. We just have to make sure that anti-free-speech Leftists don't take over the Congress of the United States and then have one of their own ascend to the White House. I shake a few hands and go home, feeling pretty good about my performance.

AN ELECTION AWAY

But time marches on and situations change. The Democrats now control both houses of Congress. Many of those Democrats now in power look with favor on Rep. Slaughter's MEDIA ACT and would not hesitate to plunge us right back into the days of regulation. If they gain enough seats, they might override the veto of a Republican president. Or, if a liberal Democrat were to reach the White House, the Fairness Doctrine could be reinstated with nothing more than a few key appointments to the FCC.

That, of course, would make life much more difficult for people like Rush Limbaugh, Sean Hannity, Bill O'Reilly, Michael Savage, and Mark Levin, whose affiliates would then have to find liberal viewpoints for balance.

There are individuals such as Howard Dean and organizations such as Media Matters that are working behind the scenes to bring back the old regulations—perhaps with more teeth than ever before. And if that doesn't have the desired effect, there are other ways to shut people up.

The Don Imus affair, for example, showcased the power of the Rev. Al Sharpton and others to have a few seconds of on-air patter designated "hate speech." If you can accomplish that, you can get rid of the offending host altogether. Was the Imus firing a tune-up to see if other hosts can be accused of hate speech?

Perhaps. But it points out a salient truth: Those who called for the dismissal of Rosie O'Donnell for her outrageous statements on "The View" and those who'd like to see MSNBC's Keith Olbermann fired for his nightly spewing on "Countdown" had better be careful of what they wish for. The Left would throw Olbermann to the wolves in a heartbeat if it meant that conservative talk radio and TV would go down with him.

Free speech should mean free speech for all—even those points-of-view that drive you crazy. So you'll forgive us if we champion the right of Rosie and Keith and even good old Al Franken to say what they will over the airwaves. What's good for the goose is good for the gander—maybe even better. In the marketplace of ideas, conservatism will win on the merits. It's Leftist thought that must suppress the other side.

And that's precisely what the Left intends to do.

II

THE PLAN TO SILENCE CONSERVATIVES

Media reform sounds like a good cause. But the gathering that took place in Memphis, Tennessee, in January of 2007 of more than 2,000 activists turned out to be an effort to push the Democratic Party further to the left and get more "progressive" voices in the media, while proposing to use the power of the federal government to silence conservatives.

In short, triumphant liberals now want to consolidate and expand their power.

Several speakers, including Sen. Bernie Sanders and Rep. Maurice Hinchey, declared that they think Congress should use a new federal "Fairness Doctrine" to target conservative speech on television and radio.

But while conservatives are not ashamed to be conservatives, because of the popularity of their ideas about freedom, a strong military, economic growth and traditional values, the liberals at this conference wanted desperately to avoid the use of the term "liberal," apparently because of its association with failed domestic, social and foreign policies. They described themselves and their causes as "progressive."

If this conference has an impact, and the participants were called upon to put pressure on the media and Congress, we should expect increasing references to the term "progressive" in coverage of controversial liberal initiatives, including the proposed agenda for "media reform." The only question is when congressional liberals get enough nerve to aggressively push this authoritarian attempt to muzzle their political opponents.

THE SOROS CONNECTION

Sponsored by Free Press, a Massachusetts-based organization that is generously subsidized by pro-Democratic Party billionaire George Soros, the "National Conference on Media Reform" featured Bill Moyers and Jesse Jackson and Hollywood celebrities such as Danny Glover, Geena Davis and Jane Fonda.

Soros, portrayed by the major media and "progressives" funded by him as a humanitarian and philanthropist, has made billions of dollars through international financial manipulations conducted through secretive off-shore hedge funds. He was convicted of insider trading in France, one of many countries to have borne the brunt of his global financial schemes.

He spent over $26 million in the 2004 presidential campaign trying to defeat Bush and also contributed to groups that have brought Democrats to power in Congress.

His "media reform" agenda is being pursued primarily through Free Press, which has received at least $400,000 over the last several years from the Soros-funded Open Society Institute. But Soros has also poured money into groups like the Center for Investigative Reporting, the Fund for Investigative Journalism, and Investigative Reporters & Editors.

One obvious purpose of such grants is to steer the media away from investigating Soros himself. However, during one media appearance, on the CBS "60 Minutes" program, Soros acknowledged that as a 14-year-old Jewish boy in Hungary, his identity was protected and that he actually assisted in confiscating property from Jews as they were being shipped off to death camps. As an adult, he shuns pro-Israel causes and believes in accommodating the Iranian regime.

The Free Press co-founder, John Nichols, has edited such books as *Against the Beast,* a critique of the "American Empire," and shares Soros's opposition to a U.S. foreign policy that targets emerging threats in the Arab/Muslim world.

In addition to the creation of what he calls a "New World Order" under U.N. auspices, Soros's causes include abortion, drug legalization, and special rights for immigrants, homosexuals, felons, and prostitutes. An atheist, Soros is promoting the complete breakdown of traditional values and morality in America.

In the official conference program, however, there was no mention of the Soros role in funding Free Press. However, thanks were extended to the Nathan Cummings Foundation, the Overbrook Foundation, Quixote Foundation, Glaser Progress Foundation, and the Haas Trusts.

"We are grateful also for the generosity and support of many other public charities, private foundations and individual donors," the conference program said, carefully concealing their identities.

Publications and organizations given credit for promoting the event included The American Prospect magazine, The Washington Monthly, The Nation, and MoveOn.org.

REDS NOT UNDER BEDS

The Revolutionary Communist Party (RCP), which opposes the Chinese communist government as too capitalist, was one of the official exhibitors. Also on hand, displaying banners calling for the impeachment of President Bush, was the so-called 9/11 truth movement, which holds that Muslims were blamed for the 2001 terrorist attacks on New York City and the Pentagon when U.S. officials actually carried them out.

Other exhibitors included the Newspaper Guild, Consumers Union, Mother Jones magazine, Pacifica Radio, and Amy Goodman, host of "Democracy Now."

While the Democratic Party and its political leaders were embraced by most of the participants and usually met with standing ovations, the official conference bookstore didn't offer any books by or about Hillary Clinton. I was told by the bookstore owner that that she was perceived as too conservative by this crowd and that those books wouldn't sell.

On the other hand, books by Senator Barack Obama and Al Gore were prominently featured. Books by Noam Chomsky, Howard Zinn, Mikhail Gorbachev, former White House reporter Helen Thomas, and Webster Tarpley, a former associate of Lyndon LaRouche, were also available. Tarpley, an "expert" on how 9/11 was a U.S. plot, was a featured guest for two hours on Air America, the liberal radio network now in bankruptcy because of bad management and dismal ratings.

A special screening of the film "Reel Bad Arabs" was held, in order to argue that Arabs and Muslims deserve more favorable coverage from the media and Hollywood. The film is narrated by Jack Shaheen, who has appeared on Al-Jazeera English making charges of anti-Arab media bias.

Very little was said during various panels about the Islamic terrorists who killed almost 3,000 Americans on 9/11 and are currently killing American soldiers and innocent civilians, most of them Muslims, in Iraq. Instead, Bush was blamed for the violence there.

Showing where conference participants stood on the matter of maintaining a U.S. military to defend America against the global Jihad, one of the books on sale at the official conference bookstore was titled, *10 Excellent Reasons Not To Join The Military.*

Former conservative David Brock, of another Soros-funded group, Media Matters, labeled the Bush foreign policy of liberating Arab lands as "criminally insane." On the same panel with Brock, Norman Solomon of the Institute for Public Accuracy suggested that U.S. foreign policy was immoral and that the media were working hand-in-glove with the Bush Administration to prepare a military attack on Iran, just as they had done with Iraq.

Reaching new levels of hysteria, Rep. Maurice Hinchey said the survival of America was itself at stake because "neo-fascist" and "neo-con" talk-show hosts led by Rush Limbaugh had facilitated the "illegal" war in Iraq and were complicit in President Bush's repeated violations of the Constitution, such as by detaining terrorists. He warned that the "right-wing oriented media" were now preparing the way for Bush to wage war on Iran and Syria.

His answer, a bill titled the "Media Ownership Reform Act," would reinstate the federal Fairness Doctrine and authorize bureaucrats at the

Federal Communications Commission (FCC) to monitor and alter the content of radio and television programs.

Hinchey, chairman of the "Future of American Media Caucus" in the House, was introduced as the new chairman of a subcommittee with jurisdiction over the FCC. For Hinchey and the vast majority at the conference, there was a pressing need for more, not less, regulation of what they call the "corporate media."

With passage of his bill, Hinchey said that "progressives" would be able to demand and get "equal access" to programs hosted by conservatives and rebut the "baloney" of people like Limbaugh. "All of that stuff will end," Hinchey said about the influence of conservative media. By name, he also denounced Fox News and Sinclair Broadcasting.

Hinchey praised Democratic FCC commissioners Michael Copps and Jonathan Adelstein, who appeared at the conference, and indicated that with the election of a Democratic president in 2008, the FCC could be openly used to frustrate the growing popularity of conservative ideas, perhaps under the cover of resisting "media consolidation."

Later, Hinchey was seen preparing for an appearance on Air America, which had a make-shift studio set up on the premises of the conference.

PROTECTING PUBLIC BROADCASTING

Democratic Rep. Steve Cohen, who was just elected to Congress from Memphis, assured the audience that Democrats would protect and possibly increase funding for public broadcasting, which he noted is on the "left hand side of the dial" but has been having problems generating listeners and viewers.

One of the cries of some participants was to "put the public back into public broadcasting," apparently a plea for even more "public" money from Congress.

Public broadcasting's Bill Moyers, who spoke to the conference about the "ravenous" nature of "Big Media," was obviously not referring to public TV or radio's appetite for U.S. tax dollars, even though AIM has documented how these entities have received over $8 billion from the taxpayers since their creation. The far-left Pacifica Radio, another taxpayer-supported network, had a heavy presence at the "media reform" conference.

The appearance of Moyers, who served as White House press secretary in the Lyndon Johnson Administration before he worked for CBS News and public TV, was curious, at least at this conference in Memphis, because he had been aware at the time of his service to LBJ of secret surveillance of Martin Luther King, Jr.

King was assassinated in Memphis in 1968 and his birthday celebration on January 15 was mentioned by several speakers, most notably Jesse Jackson, a former King aide.

One 9/11 truth movement booth featured a poster claiming that King was murdered as the result of a U.S. Government conspiracy, even though James Earl Ray was convicted of the crime and sentenced to prison. Ray died in 1998.

Continuing this fascination with conspiracy theories about the deaths of prominent people, a book for sale at the conference bookstore, titled, *American Assassination: The Strange Death of Paul Wellstone*, claims that the airplane accident that took the life of the liberal senator from Minnesota was actually deliberate murder. The book claims Wellstone's "progressive" stands made him a target.

Sen. Sanders, the only open socialist in Congress, accused the media of covering up King's opposition to the Vietnam War. He did not mention that King took that approach because he had come under the influence of identified top members of the Soviet-funded Communist Party USA, who had become his close advisers. This is one of the reasons why the Johnson Administration—and then-Attorney General Bobby Kennedy—approved FBI surveillance of him.

King's radical turn to the left, which detracts from the good work that he did, should not be a taboo topic, but it is one of many issues that "progressives" want censored from the media. Another King controversy that is off the table for "progressives" is his well-documented plagiarism.

SOCIALIST URGES ONE-SIDED COVERAGE

Sanders, who votes with the Democrats in the Senate despite his official status as an independent socialist, claimed conservatives were

99 percent in control of talk radio and that it was time "to open the question of the Fairness Doctrine again" to restrict what they say and how they say it.

He faulted the media for covering two sides of the global warming debate "when there is no debate in the scientific community."

Clearly, therefore, the purpose in proposing a "fairness doctrine" is not to offer different points of view but to silence viewpoints liberals regard as unsound or unpopular.

Sanders indicated he would introduce a Senate version of the Hinchey bill.

A similar bill, the "Fairness in Broadcasting Act," was sponsored by Democratic Rep. Louise Slaughter, the chairman of the House Rules Committee that has enormous influence over what bills are brought up for votes.

The Rev. Jesse Jackson, the object of fawning media coverage despite the scandal of producing a child from an extramarital affair, argued before the conference for "the right to be heard" and insisted that the major media were not telling the real story of pain and suffering in George Bush's America.

Despite claiming to be for open debate and discussion, he recently urged consumers to boycott DVDs of the Seinfeld comedy show because the actor who plays one of the characters had been caught making racist comments in a nightclub. Jackson had the actor, Michael Richards, on his radio show to apologize for the remarks.

Suggesting the real agenda behind "media reform," Jackson said that the key to Democrats winning "is more access to the media."

That may depend, however, on how the "progressives" market their unpopular ideas, especially when they actively begin their congressional campaign of suppressing viewpoints in opposition to their own.

Making himself out to be a victim, Jackson said that he should be called by the media for comments on foreign policy issues like Iraq, rather than just racial controversies like the Duke rape case.

Clearly staking out a position on the far-left fringe, Jackson accused Democratic House Speaker Nancy Pelosi of taking "baby steps" legislatively when she should be exercising "bold leadership." On Iraq, he said, "you can't be against the war and for the war budget." Rather than just raise the minimum wage, he said Pelosi should introduce a massive new jobs program. He concluded his remarks by asking people to watch his TV program on the Word television network and to tune into his "Keep Hope Alive" radio show on 50 stations.

REPUBLICANS AS THIEVES

At a panel moderated by Paul Waldman of Media Matters, Steve Freeman of the University of Pennsylvania argued that the 2004 presidential election was stolen on behalf of George W. Bush. His associate, Jonathan Simon of the Election Defense Alliance, took to the microphone during the question-and-answer period to argue that the 2006 elections were rigged as well and that the Republicans are preparing to steal the 2008 presidential election. Waldman, who claimed to be dedicated to factual accuracy in covering current events, didn't dispute any of this. In fact, he stated his belief that Al Gore had won the 2000 election and that the media knew it.

Another panelist, Cornell Belcher, the official pollster for the Democratic National Committee, seemed to be taken aback by the conspiracy theories and pointed out that the Democrats had, in fact, made substantial gains on the federal and state levels in 2006.

However, during a conversation over breakfast, Freeman reiterated his belief that the Democrats had won far more seats than they were given credit for in 2006. Asked why they wouldn't protest the stealing of votes, he said, "Democrats are in on it." He described Republicans and Democrats as the A team and B team, and that when one team makes too many mistakes, the other goes in for relief. Asked for his opinion on the 9/11 truth movement, he said, "Nothing would surprise me."

A panel on "Media, War, and Impeachment" featured Jeff Cohen, founder of Fairness and Accuracy in Reporting (FAIR), whose December 2006 magazine features Hugo Chavez of Venezuela on the cover as he addressed the U.N. holding up a copy of Noam Chomsky's book on the dangers of American "hegemony." That was the appearance in which Chavez labeled Bush the devil.

The article inside the magazine by FAIR's Steve Rendall accused the American media of unfairly criticizing Chavez for "challenging the U.S.," not because he makes absurd charges, chums around with people such as the anti-Semitic and anti-American Iranian president, and threatens press freedom in his own country. Promising "Socialism or death," Chavez had just been sworn in for another presidential term. As participants prepared for an event featuring Jane Fonda, they were given copies of a four-page flier advertising Bob Avakian's book, *From Ike to Mao and Beyond.* The flier said that Avakian, the leader of the Revolutionary Communist Party, has been described by Cornell West of Princeton University as "a long distance runner in the freedom struggle against imperialism, racism and capitalism."

Scott Lee, an RCP "helper" passing out the fliers, told me that he thought the conference was worthwhile but too heavily tilted in favor of the Democratic Party. He said he wasn't aware that global capitalist George Soros had funded the left-wing conference organizers but that the money had gone for a good cause.

This is what passes for "progressivism" these days. It is a clear danger to freedom at home and abroad.

The Fairness Doctrine would put bureaucrats from the Federal Communications Commission in charge of managing editorial content on radio and TV networks, channels and stations.

The organized left-wing campaign against Fox News, in order to keep Democratic presidential candidates out of any debates sponsored or co-sponsored by the channel, is a taste of what is to come. The left-wing campaign against Fox News is one reason why the channel hired former liberal Democratic Congressman Harold Ford, Jr. as a commentator and analyst. In fact, Ford had been a favorite of the channel during his run for the Senate, and he had received campaign contributions from Rupert Murdoch, chairman of the Fox News parent company, and other News Corporation executives. The channel has been feeling the heat.

Of course, the notion that the channel is a conservative Republican mouthpiece is completely absurd and is offered only for the purpose of intimidating its executives and news personalities and moving it further to the left. AIM has put forward a very detailed critique of the channel on conservative grounds, noting its timid coverage of Senator

Hillary Clinton and its backing away from asking important questions about Senator Barack Obama's mysterious past.

This brings up the other serious problem that we face—self-censorship. Tragically, the conservative media, which we now depend on for alternative news and information, have been very disappointing in their coverage of a number of key controversies and issues of public importance. In the face of a campaign to return the Fairness Doctrine, the natural reaction of many in the conservative media might be to bend over backwards to an even greater degree, in order to accommodate the left.

NORTH AMERICAN UNION

One example is the reaction to evidence that U.S. officials are laying the groundwork for a North American entity, sometimes called a "North American Community" or "North American Union" of the U.S., Canada and Mexico in economic and other spheres. I attended a Washington conference devoted to developing a North American legal system that included literature outlining the creation of a North American Supreme Court. Lou Dobbs of CNN had me on his show to talk about it. "It's clear that you're as astounded as I am and as my colleagues are that more people in the media are not focusing on this issue," he said. Indeed, it is a story with dramatic implications for the survival of our nation as a sovereign entity. Yet, Dobbs is the only major media figure to consider the issue newsworthy.

Judicial Watch, the public interest law firm, uncovered federal documents indicating that secretive "working groups" in the Security and Prosperity Partnership (SPP), a Bush Administration initiative, are working on a "One Card" concept to facilitate cross-border movement among the three countries. The SPP is being sold to the public as an attempt to help business, but the documents indicate a far-reaching effort to erase national borders and even national identity. Previous documents released by Judicial Watch through the Freedom of Information Act reveal a strategy called "evolution by stealth" to undermine the sovereignty of the three countries. That suggests a determined effort to keep this from the American people.

It may be difficult for the rest of the media to continue ignoring the controversy because opposition to the SPP is growing not only in the U.S. but Canada and Mexico.

GLOBAL WARMING

Global warming is another story that gets pathetic coverage. Leading liberals such as Senator Bernie Sanders and Robert F. Kennedy, Jr. have openly stated that the debate over global warming is over and that the media have an obligation to report that only one side is based on science. In Kennedy's case, he was actually hired by the Fox News Channel to host a one-sided special on global warming. We are constantly told about a supposed "consensus" in favor of the man-made global warming theory but the fact is that 18,000 Americans with university degrees in physical science have signed a petition declaring that there is no convincing scientific evidence that the human release of carbon dioxide, methane or other greenhouse gasses is causing catastrophic heating of the Earth's atmosphere and disruption of the Earth's climate. One of the signers, Dr. Arthur Robinson, editor of the highly informative Access to Energy newsletter, calls the claimed scientific consensus in favor of the man-made global warming theory "an outright lie."

GAY RIGHTS

Coverage of "gay rights" is another terrible blemish on the national press. All major U.S. papers support gay marriage and even run announcements of same. The influence of the Gay & Lesbian Alliance Against Defamation (GLAAD), which enforces conformity in the media on this issue, helps explain why it is rare to find objective coverage of the movement that exists in the U.S. and other countries of thousands of former homosexuals. Alan Chambers, the former homosexual who runs Exodus International, tries to interest the media in the fact that true change from homosexuality is possible and that people have experienced and can talk about true change. Chambers says he employs a full-time communications specialist to reach out to the media but that the Fox News Channel has "never responded" and shows no interest. In general, he adds, the media have a pro-homosexual slant, although he did find Lester Holt of NBC News and Anderson Cooper of CNN to be fair in their handling of the controversy.

Chambers tells AIM that he is troubled by the practice of national news organizations giving money to the National Lesbian and Gay Journalists Association (NLGJA). All major news organizations, including Fox News, have given grants to NLGJA. Chambers recalls an official of the group advising the press not to cover former homosexuals because it would be comparable to quoting the Ku Klux Klan about civil rights. That is the mind-set that guides the media on this matter.

THE AIDS THEORY

In a related matter, questions about the HIV/AIDS theory are not considered worthy of media attention, even though the U.S. has spent about $200 billion on HIV/AIDS and an AIDS vaccine since 1981 without a cure being found. An international organization of more than 2,300 scientists, medical doctors, journalists, health advocates and business professionals has formed "Rethinking AIDS," in order to raise those questions. Among other things, it points out that the definition of AIDS in Africa does not require HIV testing and that symptoms of a disease said to be AIDS are compatible with symptoms of malnutrition. As such, critics of the AIDS theory argue that "AIDS in Africa" should be fought with a campaign to raise living standards, not force controversial and potentially toxic anti-AIDS drugs on the populace. Nevertheless, an international airline tax is now being collected to buy and distribute these controversial drugs to people around the world, especially in Africa. The campaign is being waged with the backing of the United Nations.

On this matter, the Fox News website did perform a public service, running a column in 2005 by Jonathan M. Fishbein on how he uncovered widespread scientific and professional misconduct at the National Institutes of Health Division of AIDS. Fishbein, whose case is the subject of the Honest Doctor website, charges that the agency "knowingly and cunningly covered up evidence of shoddy conduct in a trial examining the safety and efficacy of [anti-AIDS drug] nevirapine to prevent the maternal-to-child ("vertical") transmission of the deadly AIDS virus." Yet a Google search will disclose very few stories in the major media about the Fishbein allegations.

EVOLUTION VS. INTELLIGENT DESIGN

Like the AIDS and man-made global warming theories, Darwin's theory of evolution is another accepted truth, as far as most of the media are concerned. The emerging scientific theory of intelligent design is typically panned by the media as religious in nature. The Discovery Institute maintains a blog completely devoted to misreporting of the evolution issue, documenting how "much of the news coverage has been sloppy, inaccurate, and in some cases, overtly biased." The bias was reflected in the non-coverage, in December of 2004, of atheist philosopher Antony Flew's pronouncement that advancements in science, especially in DNA research, had convinced him of the existence of God.

MORE, NOT LESS, INFORMATION

Whatever one may think of these various issues and controversies, there are two legitimate sides to the debates and yet many national news organizations have decided to either ignore them or cover only one side. These are not insignificant or trivial matters. They concern profound issues of national and global importance that affect our lives and our country.

Under the circumstances, a federal Fairness Doctrine sounds appealing but we know that it is an initiative that is designed mainly to give "progressives" even more access to the media and increase the power they already exercise. Conservatives have to remain committed to freedom of speech and freedom of information while increasing their own pressure on the liberal and conservative media to be truly "fair and balanced."

III

THE RISE OF
THE NEW MEDIA

BY LYNN WOOLLEY

The Left just can't give it up.

Once you've had a virtual monopoly on the airwaves, it's difficult to deal with a new landscape in which anyone can express a political opinion about anything without fear of regulation or retribution.

But that's what happened to the Left.

One morning, they woke up and heard things on the radio that they'd never heard before. It was shocking. How could an ex-disc jockey named Rush Limbaugh say these things? And then the info-gods seemed to just pile on. First it was talk radio; then cable TV came along with its glut of nightly talk shows. Larry King never offended anyone on the Left, but then that @#$%^&* Fox News Channel signed on and suddenly there was even more divergence of opinion. Bill O'Reilly, Sean Hannity, John Gibson.

Sure the Left believed that "our strength is our diversity." But NOT in the area of political thought. In that arena, the left surely believed that diversity was no strength at all. The Left had owned the major media to the extent that the rare conservative commentator was always labeled—as in "well-known CONSERVATIVE William F.

Buckley." It was a given that the usual commentator was liberal and therefore mainstream.

How things have changed!

And how the Left would like to undo those changes.

To fully understand what the Left has lost, you must look at the situation from their point of view:

Imagine a football game in which all the media supported the same team, and in which the favored squad was always given a shorter length of field. That doesn't seem fair, and yet—in the name of fairness— that is precisely the situation that existed for years in the media.

The "Fairness Doctrine," a name that only Herbert Marcuse could love, wasn't really even a law. It was just a regulation of the Federal Communications Commission (FCC) that required broadcast stations to present political issues in an honest, equal, and balanced manner.

The Fairness Doctrine came into being in 1949 and lasted until the Reagan administration. During that period, and up until 1987 when Rush Limbaugh started his talk show on KFBK in Sacramento, the three traditional networks enjoyed a virtual monopoly on political thought over the airwaves.

POWERFUL UNCLE WALTER

Since news programming was exempted from the regulation, the networks could air whatever they pleased with no requirement for equal time or even balance. Because of that, the networks enjoyed tremendous power to frame issues in whatever manner they pleased and to influence public opinion.

When CBS' Walter Cronkite editorialized during the Tet Offensive that the Vietnam War was unwinnable, President Lyndon Johnson famously said, "If I've lost Walter Cronkite, I've lost Middle America." History surely changed when Johnson declined to run for reelection.

What power the networks had!

And since news was exempt from the Doctrine, political office-holders had a near lock on coverage. Incumbent senators and House members make lots of news; challengers do not. And remember, there was no Rush or Sean or Fox News Channel to interview the Tom Tancredos of the day.

The signs are there for anyone who cares to notice them—emerging indications and even threats that it's time for government to tamper with broadcast freedom of speech once again. Many in the Democratic Party are now openly discussing their distaste with Mr. Limbaugh's continued popularity, the Fox News Channel, and the abject failure of attempts to establish a liberal foothold in talk radio. There's a feeling among liberals that something must be done.

APPROVED THINKING

When you analyze liberalism and how it works, you begin to realize that it flourishes in an atmosphere of intimidation. Certain ways of thinking become approved and are added to the liberal canon; wrong thinking is then punished, or the wrong thinker is ostracized. The modern term for this type of mental intimidation is "Political Correctness."

It is no accident that the PC movement coalesced on our college campuses. Liberal thought has long dominated academia, all the way from kindergarten to graduate school. So colleges and universities became the breeding ground for this new, "progressive" outlook on life. The movement is easily spread into other liberal communities such as the national news media, Hollywood, and the Democratic Party. (Among the items that are PC: radical environmentalism, feminism, abortion, multiculturalism and homosexuality. Among those items that are not PC: prayer and religion, business, guns, and tax cuts.)

You'll notice here that the PC movement controls most of the input into young minds including movies, the music they hear on the radio, and their teachers. Teenagers and young adults aren't exposed to the usual sources of non-PC material such as the Wall Street Journal, Paul Harvey in his heyday and—well, Investor's Business Daily. (It was hard to come up with three sources.) But with the abandonment of the Fairness Doctrine, an entire new world of thought and opinion opened up! Talk show hosts actually challenged the status quo and dared to disagree.

When the Fairness Doctrine was abolished—free speech on the radio blossomed and led to the emergence of two towering figures: Rush Limbaugh and Dr. Laura Schlessinger.

The PC crowd had a problem. Suddenly there were opposition voices in the fields of politics (Rush) and human relationships (Dr. Laura) and the audiences were large and growing. Young people were tuning in. The mainstream media and Hollywood still had its influence, but now, there was a small chink in the armor. More chinks began to appear until the broadcast landscape was cluttered with a virtual cornucopia of points of view. Rush represented a sort of "mainstream" of conservative thought and begat hundreds of imitators at the national and local levels. Hard-hitting conservatives like Michael Savage and Mark Levin appeared on the scene to mercilessly lambaste liberals. Religious broadcasters got into the act, and created entire networks to broadcast conservatives with faith-based backgrounds like Michael Medved and Dennis Pager. But these hosts were not doing overt religious shows; they were heavily into politics and popular culture—a direct counter to the liberalism of academia. And, of course, outright religious broadcasters such as Dr. James Dobson of "Focus on the Family" were empowered to enter the political field as well—and they became more popular and began to exert tremendous influence.

As If Free Speech on Radio Isn't Bad Enough

To the Left, the situation on cable television is almost as bad. When the cable landscape was dominated by CNN, the viewing public had little more than a 24-hour version of the Big Three networks' evening newscast. Larry King, a pioneer of today's nightly cable talk shows, was no conservative, and rarely asked hard questions. The Clintons were frequent guests and could appear on King's show without fear of challenge.

But then came Fox News Channel and suddenly, as in the rise of political talk on radio, there was a divergence of opinion on television screens. Bill O'Reilly was not afraid to rock the boat, and though not as conservative as Limbaugh, he often attacked what he saw as corruptness or ineptness of those in office. Many of his targets were liberals. Add to that the fact that a young broadcaster named Sean Hannity had been teamed up with a radio liberal named Alan Colmes—and that Hannity seemed to be the star of the show—and the Left was reduced to making charges that Fox News Channel was an arm of the Republican Party.

You'd think that no Fairness Doctrine would be necessary in the case of cable talk, right? After all, CNN, with the exception of "Lou Dobbs Tonight" features virtually nothing in the way of conservative opinion, and Mr. Dobbs' conservatism is largely related to one issue—immigration. The other cable news outlet, MSNBC, has made an effort to position itself as the liberal cable network. Its top stars, Chris Matthews and Keith Olbermann, are both products of the Left; in fact, Olbermann is a flaming liberal. But MSNBC's audience is miniscule in relation to that of Fox. Liberal logic dictates that if no one is watching MSNBC's talk shows, then Fox's talk shows should be regulated. Go figure.

HUSH RUSH AND BILL-O, TOO

The rise of the New Media has been underway for more than two decades now, and the Left has had its fill.

In the nineties, Democrats made an attempt to correct the situation with a new Fairness Doctrine known as the "Hush Rush" legislation. It failed. A Gore presidency might have led to another attempt had the hanging chads in Florida not gotten in his way.

One thing that separates liberals from conservatives is that liberals are craftier and work without the hindrance of a conscience. They always think that they are right, and any means to achieve the end is acceptable. They are tired of dealing with Limbaugh, Hannity, Levin, Laura, and conservative talk in general. If they can return to the way things used to be, they will do it.

The fact that the public in general seems unaware of continued efforts to reinstate the Fairness Doctrine doesn't mean it isn't happening.

Since 1985 when FCC Chairman Mark S. Fowler announced that the Doctrine violated the First Amendment and harmed the public interest, the Left has been in a state of denial. They believed that the constitutionality of the Doctrine would ultimately be upheld as it had been in Red Lion Broadcasting Co. v. FCC in 1969. And since 1987, when the Doctrine DID go away, the Left has never stopped trying to bring it back.

In that very year, Congress tried to contest the FCC's abandonment of the regulation. Legislation to fully restore the Doctrine made it to President Ronald Reagan's desk, and he promptly vetoed it. Another attempt to bring back the Doctrine in 1991 failed when President George H.W. Bush made it known that he, too, would veto such a measure.

"The Fairness in Broadcasting Act of 1993," sponsored by Ernest Hollings (D-SC) in the Senate and Bill Hefner (D-NC) in the House, would have placed the Doctrine into law, but it went nowhere.

As of 2007, Sen. Bernie Sanders (I-VT), Rep. Dennis Kucinich (D-OH), and Rep. Maurice Hinchey (D-NY) are announced supporters of returning the Doctrine. But perhaps the most up-front proponent is Congresswoman Louise Slaughter (D-NY) whose MEDIA ACT (HR 4710) would reinstate the Fairness Doctrine and "ensure that broadcasters present discussions of conflicting views on issues of public importance."

"Fairness isn't going to hurt anybody," she says. "I just can't imagine these people who want to fight against fairness."

As long as the political Left can use a law based on the Fairness Doctrine, and then later the courts, to decide what is fair and what isn't, Congresswoman Slaughter would presumably be happy.

What's fair would be precisely what's fair to her.

It's a matter of time. And elections.

The Left has never gotten over the fact that it once had a media monopoly. It hates the New Media, particularly talk radio, and can't understand why so many people tune in. As Hillary Clinton once opined, it must be due to some "vast right-wing conspiracy."

Under Republican presidents, efforts to restore government regulation that might allow the courts to decide fairness have failed.

Attempts to counter conservative talk radio with liberal talk shows (Air America) failed. Nobody listened to the liberal comedians that served as hosts.

The "Hate Radio" movement has achieved moderate success, but the highest-profile victim, Don Imus, was not a conservative. Still, this tactic shows some promise, especially in light of Rush's parody of "Obama the Magic Negro."

But the best way for the Left to restore liberal balance to the airwaves remains the ballot box. One is hard-pressed to think that any of the Democratic presidential frontrunners—particularly Hillary Clinton or Al Gore if he should enter the race—would not enthusiastically support the return of the Fairness Doctrine.

The Democrats are two-thirds of the way back to regulation. All they need is the White House.

IV

HISTORY OF THE FAIRNESS DOCTRINE

BY CLIFF KINCAID

In his classic work about Washington double-standards that benefit the national Democratic Party, *It Didn't Start With Watergate,* Victor Lasky described how Democratic administrations were guilty of some of the same things that forced the resignation of Republican President Richard Nixon, such as the use of "dirty tricks" against the opposition and compiling an "enemies list" of media critics.

In one notorious case, Lasky noted that the federal Fairness Doctrine was used by the Kennedy and Johnson Administrations as part of a coordinated covert campaign, using front groups and money from the Democratic National Committee, to go after "right-wing critics in the broadcast media," particularly during the 1964 presidential campaign. "It was a conspiracy, pure and simple," Lasky notes, "one which was aimed at curbing free expression."

This time, the "conspiracy" is out in the open. All of the progress that conservatives have made in the media over the last several decades is now in jeopardy.

"MEDIA REFORM"

At the Memphis, Tennessee, "National Conference on Media Reform," underwritten by billionaire George Soros and rich liberal foundations, powerful liberal members of Congress, led by Socialist Senator Bernie Sanders and Rep. Maurice Hinchey, outlined a plan to pass a new version of the so-called Fairness Doctrine targeting conservative media. Thousands of "progressive" activists were asked to build grassroots support for passage of the bill and the two current Democratic members of the Federal Communications Commission (FCC), Michael J. Copps and Jonathan S. Adelstein, were in attendance and spoke. Copps and Adelstein can be counted on to vote to bring back the Fairness Doctrine.

Some experts say that the FCC has the power to re-impose the doctrine without congressional or executive action. One said, however, that it would have to make a factual case that the Fairness Doctrine is not only needed but would not violate the First Amendment rights of broadcasters. Such a rationale would be needed because the FCC had found that the Fairness Doctrine was no longer needed (to ensure diversity of viewpoints) and that it violated broadcasters' First Amendment rights. Making the contrary case today—with 900-channel cable, direct broadcast satellite, Sirius/XM satellite radio, podcasts, and the Internet, would be difficult but not impossible.

With a Democratic president, the FCC would have a 3-2 Democratic majority, capable of re-imposing the Fairness Doctrine on its own. Under the law, the FCC is directed by five Commissioners appointed by the president and confirmed by the Senate for 5-year terms, except when filling an unexpired term. The president designates one of the Commissioners to serve as Chairperson and only three Commissioners may be members of the same political party.

Perceiving a threat to their First Amendment rights, opponents of the Fairness Doctrine are mobilizing. The National Religious Broadcasters, on February 16, 2007, passed a resolution noting that the Fairness Doctrine had "a chilling and stifling effect on broadcasters and programmers" but that "the new leadership of the U.S. Congress has signaled a propensity toward reinstating the 'Fairness Doctrine" during the upcoming 110th Congress." The NRB said it "strongly opposes any attempt to reinstate or make the 'Fairness Doctrine' the law of the land and further pledges to vigorously oppose any such action."

The American Center for Law and Justice (ACLJ) has declared that the Fairness Doctrine "would have a significant and serious impact on Christian broadcasting." Jay Sekulow, chief counsel for the ACLJ, says that, under the Fairness Doctrine, "…the proclamation of the Gospel, the definition of marriage and the issue of abortion would all be deemed 'controversial topics'" that require giving airtime to opposing views. Sekulow, who hosts his own show, adds that "Under this blatant form of compelled speech, broadcasters who air "Jay Sekulow Live!" or "Focus on the Family" with Dr. [James] Dobson could be compelled to run a counter-viewpoint to the positions we just advocated. Therefore, Christian broadcasters would be put in the uncomfortable position of having to air positions that violate their conscience and sincerely held religious beliefs."

Soros Calls Hinchey's Tune

Hinchey, the founder and chairman of the Future of American Media Caucus, is one of many liberal members of Congress who receive campaign contributions from George Soros. Hinchey has joined with Democratic Reps. Lynn Woolsey, Tammy Baldwin, and Marcy Kaptur in calling on the major television networks (ABC, CBS, NBC, and Fox) to address the findings of a Media Matters for America study purporting to show that Republican and conservative voices were "dominating the influential Sunday-morning talk shows." Media Matters, also subsidized by Soros, is headed by David Brock, a former conservative and closeted homosexual who wrote a book that was so soft on Hillary Clinton that it bombed.

Brock claims that the perception of liberal media bias is the result of a Republican spin or "noise" machine that has to be silenced. But when he made that claim on a CNBC program, another guest, Newsweek senior writer Charles Gasparino, was flabbergasted. Gasparino explained, "We sow the seeds of our own demise. Journalists have been advocates of the liberal attitude for way too long, and now we're paying the price—Fox News."

Gasparino was saying something that should be quite obvious—that Fox News, the most successful cable news network, is a response to the overwhelming liberal media bias. Gasparino said, "Journalists are generally liberal. That does come out in the reporting...It comes out in the stories that they do." Ignoring the abundant evidence of the liberal media bias which gave rise to Fox News, Brock and his Capitol Hill collaborators, like Hinchey, want the public to believe the problem is Fox News and other "conservative" media.

Left-wing "progressive" activists forced the Democratic Party to abandon plans to hold a presidential debate under the sponsorship of Fox News Channel (FNC), on the pretext that FNC was too conservative and that Democrats should not be associating with such a news organization. One activist, Robert Greenwald of Brave New Films, who did the film, *Outfoxed,* urged Democrats not even to appear on the channel. FNC responded to the pressure by announcing the hiring of former liberal Democratic Rep. Harold Ford, Jr., a close associate of Senator Hillary Clinton, as a Fox News analyst and commentator. Rupert Murdoch, chairman of the Fox News parent company, News Corporation, contributed to the Hillary Clinton for Senate campaign and his New York Post newspaper endorsed her.

One of the complaints from the critics of Fox News was that allegations in a story published by the on-line Insight magazine were repeated on the air by Fox News. The story was that Hillary Clinton operatives were looking into Senator and presidential candidate Barack Obama's alleged attendance at a radical Islamic school in Indonesia, a mostly Muslim country where he was raised.

The "progressives" were angry the subject was even mentioned. One liberal paper, the Freeport (Illinois) Journal-Standard, declared that "while few read Insight, the lie quickly spread to the talk radio instigators, who repeated it ad nauseam, with no equal time given to opposing views, much less the truth." The paper said restoration of the Fairness Doctrine would rein in the "partisan noise machine" that targets Democrats.

But the story was never proven to be a lie, and legitimate questions remain about Obama's Muslim past. It is certainly the case that "progressives" wanted to use this controversy to make conservative media pay for running the story. Lacking a fairness doctrine, Cenk Uygur on the Huffington Post website suggested the use of liberal political pressure, such as a refusal by Democratic Party politicians to appear on Fox News or a boycott of the channel's advertisers. Ironically, the Huffington Post had treated Insight magazine as a legitimate source of political news in the past.

Clearly, what the organized left wants to accomplish is the intimidation of the media, especially Fox News, into not reporting on news items embarrassing to the Democrats. They desperately want to keep Fox News in line because the channel has been, on occasion, a source of news and information that people can't find anywhere else. Except for Fox News, for example, there has been no coverage of Obama's membership in a black nationalist church.

The pressure worked in this case. After first defending the coverage of the Insight story, Fox News vice president Bill Shine said that his channel "gave too much credence" to it and "spent far too long discussing its premise on the air." The left-wing critics of Fox News had scored a victory. The Fairness Doctrine holds out the hope for these activists of using the federal government to further intimidate the channel.

In regard to the other leading Democratic presidential candidate, Senator Clinton, it is not reassuring to reflect upon the fact that Fox News gave little attention to the explosive book, *The Truth About Hillary*, by Edward Klein, which raised questions about Senator Clinton's "sexual preference," or lifestyle. Like Obama's Muslim past, this is a taboo topic for the "progressive" left.

A similar left-wing pressure campaign was launched against the Congressional Black Caucus Institute for announcing that it would partner with FNC to co-host presidential debates. The campaign wanted all Democratic presidential candidates to avoid the debate on Fox and instead to appear on one sponsored by CNN.

THE SORDID HISTORY

The use of the Fairness Doctrine for partisan political purposes, including intimidation and harassment, was documented in Fred Friendly's 1975 book, *The Good Guys, the Bad Guys and the First Amendment*. Friendly, a president of CBS news who became the Edward R.

Murrow Professor of Journalism at the Columbia School of Journalism, shows how Kennedy and Johnson Administration officials, working with Democratic congressional staffers, the Democratic National Committee, and a liberal journalist by the name of Fred Cook, countered the influence of and even silenced conservative radio personalities. Bill Ruder, a Kennedy Administration official, admitted, "Our massive strategy was to use the Fairness Doctrine to challenge and harass right-wing broadcasters and hope that the challenges would be so costly to them that they would be inhibited and decide it was too expensive to continue."

A similar strategy is being used today, even without an actual Fairness Doctrine in place. Indeed, during the 2004 presidential campaign, many of the same groups seeking the return of the Fairness Doctrine pressured Sinclair Broadcasting to drop plans to air a 90-minute documentary critical of John Kerry. The film, *Stolen Honor: Wounds That Never Heal,* was about Kerry's anti-Vietnam war activity contributing to the torture of our POWs. The film was going to air on all of Sinclair's 62 stations, reaching 25 percent of the nation's households, many of them in voter "swing" states before the election.

In a letter to the FCC, 19 Democratic Senators called the film "an anti-Kerry attack ad" and insisted that its airing would represent an improper use of the public airwaves and might "violate fairness rules now in place." The 19 Democratic Senators were Dianne Feinstein, Ted Kennedy, Patrick Leahy, Frank R. Lautenberg, Byron Dorgan, Dick Durbin, Jack Reed, Tim Johnson, Bill Nelson, Harry Reid, Debbie Stabenow, Carl Levin, Daniel Inouye, Ron Wyden, Blanche Lincoln, Bob Graham, Fritz Hollings, Patty Murray, and Mark Pryor.

FCC commissioner Copps was also critical of Sinclair, saying, "This is an abuse of the public trust…And it is proof positive of media consolidation run amok when one owner can use the public airwaves to blanket the country with its political ideology—whether liberal or conservative."

Following the controversy, Tom Athans of Democracy Radio (the husband of Democratic Senator Stabenow), David Brock of Media Matters for America, and Andrew Jay Schwartzman of the Democracy Access Project announced they were launching a campaign to bring back the Fairness Doctrine. Media Matters released a poll purporting to find that 77 percent of respondents said that TV and radio stations that use public airwaves should be required to present both sides of an issue. A Democracy Radio survey claimed that 90 percent of all broadcast hours on talk radio are fairly characterized as conservative.

Another Fairness Doctrine supporter, Steve Rendall of Fairness & Accuracy in Reporting (FAIR), wrote a piece entitled, "The Fairness Doctrine: How we lost it, and why we need it back." He noted that Robert F. Kennedy Jr., in his book, *Crimes Against Nature,* "probes the failure of broadcasters to cover the environment, " and that Kennedy wrote that "The FCC's pro-industry, anti-regulatory philosophy has effectively ended the right of access to broadcast television by any but the moneyed interests." Kennedy has also declared that "The decline in American journalism began in 1988 when Reagan abolished the Fairness Doctrine."

Yet Kennedy's viewpoint on global warming and the environment is so widely accepted by the media that even the "conservative" Fox News Channel hired him as a special correspondent to do a November 2005 special program on global warming. Kennedy said that he personally convinced Fox News chairman Roger Ailes to air the program and that they had been friends for years. Eventually, under pressure from conservatives, Fox aired another program expressing some doubts about the man-made global warming theory.

Rather than propose that the media present both sides of controversial issues of public importance, Kennedy tells student audiences that there are not two sides to the global warming debate. Obviously, he wants to bring back the Fairness Doctrine not to ensure true fairness and balance in journalism but to intimidate and censor those expressing a view contrary to his own. This is the real agenda of the radical left and the "media reform" movement.

ABC'S "THE PATH TO 9/11"

Their agenda was demonstrated when the Democratic Party and 20 senators sent letters to the FCC in protest over ABC running its "The Path to 9/11" miniseries, which aired on the nights of September 10 and 11, 2006. They regarded it as an unflattering portrait of former

President Clinton and his administration's handling of the terrorism problem. Howard Wolfson, then a senior adviser to the Democratic National Committee (and now a top adviser to Democratic Senator and presidential candidate Hillary Clinton), claimed that the program would constitute an illegal in-kind contribution to Republicans.

In a letter to Robert Iger, president and CEO of the Walt Disney Company, the parent of ABC, then-Senate Democratic Leader Harry Reid, Assistant Democratic Leader Dick Durbin, Senator Debbie Stabenow, Senator Charles Schumer, and Senator Byron Dorgan urged the Disney CEO to cancel the film, saying, "The Communications Act of 1934 provides your network with a free broadcast license predicated on the fundamental understanding of your principle obligation to act as a trustee of the public airwaves in serving the public interest. Nowhere is this public interest obligation more apparent than in the duty of broadcasters to serve the civic needs of a democracy by promoting an open and accurate discussion of political ideas and events."

The message was unmistakable: change the film to please us or face legal and congressional consequences. That was an implied threat to revoke ABC's broadcasting license unless it censored the ABC drama. The Democratic Party also urged supporters to sign petitions to Iger calling the miniseries "a bald-faced attempt to slander Democrats." Some changes to the film were made before airing.

Two weeks later, Chris Wallace, host of Fox News Sunday, was viciously attacked for grilling former President Clinton over his handling of the 9/11 terrorist attacks. Clinton told Wallace, "So you did Fox's bidding on this show. You did your nice little conservative hit job on me."

Conservative radio host Rush Limbaugh commented that, in one sense, the Democrats were acting silly, as if they were afraid of Fox News. But he saw another motive in their attacks. "These people are Stalinists," he said. "They are not going to tolerate anything that dissents from their views. It's out there and it's wide open for everybody to see."

THE CURRENT CAMPAIGN

The Free Press, the group behind the Memphis "media reform"

conference, is carefully laying the groundwork for the return of the Fairness Doctrine. It staged "Media Reform in Your Living Room" house parties around the country. Activists in charge of the house parties were provided with the following materials:

- Media Reform's Moment: Highlights from the National Conference for Media Reform DVD.
- Free Press E-Activist, Media Reform Regional and Daily sign-up sheets.
- "Stop Big Media" postcards.
- Act Now! Handouts.
- Donating to the Free Press Action Fund Talking Points.
- Free Press Action Fund Donation Forms and envelopes.

Its "Media Reform Action Guide" describes in detail how to "Launch a Targeted Campaign Against a Media Outlet." It explains:

"More effective than a single complaint, a coordinated campaign may succeed in pressuring media outlets to alter their news coverage, air a popular program, or make other changes. If you and others in your community share the same complaint about your media, join forces and ramp up the pressure."

Some of the tactics include a letter writing campaign, meetings with media management, compiling a report about the station's misbehavior and sending it to people "in authority" in your community, working with other media, distributing fliers, organizing a boycott of companies advertising on the station, and holding a demonstration in front of the station's headquarters.

It is also advised to complain to the FCC about how a station is allegedly violating FCC rules and by filing objections when TV and radio licenses are up for renewal.

The Free Press "Action Guide" urges "progressive" activists to connect with local media reform groups and cites six local and regional media activist groups. It also lists "talking points for a presentation on media reform."

In a sample letter to members of Congress, the Free Press declares that:

> "We have a Constitutional right to a media system that offers a diversity of voices over mainstream channels. We have a Constitutional right to open up the public airwaves to as many speakers as technology will permit, and a responsibility to ensure that our communications systems are open and accessible to all public speakers, great and small."

Needless to say, there is no such "Constitutional right" in the U.S. Constitution. What the Free Press is saying is that the federal government should control the media and give the "progressives" special access. This runs directly contrary to the First Amendment, which prohibits congressional interference with the right of free speech.

HISTORY REPEATS ITSELF

The Kennedy and Johnson Administrations' campaigns against conservative media may provide some indications of how the current campaign may be played out.

Key officials involved in the campaign were Kenneth O'Donnell, a trusted friend and appointment secretary of President Kennedy, and Wayne Phillips, a former reporter for the New York Times who had joined the Kennedy Administration as special assistant to the Administrator of the Housing Administration. The key Capitol Hill staffer was Nick Zapple, counsel to the Senate Communications Subcommittee, headed by Senator John O. Pastore.

A key part of their campaign was a Cook article in The Nation magazine, "Radio Right: Hate Clubs of the Air." Fred Friendly confirmed that Phillips, who later became director of News and Information for the Democratic National Committee, had proposed the article and made "major contributions" to its content. Cook also wrote a book, subsidized by the Democratic National Committee, attacking 1964 Republican presidential candidate Barry Goldwater. Another key aspect of the campaign was the use of a Washington organization known as

Group Research, Inc., which monitored right-wing publications and broadcasters and was run by a long-time Democratic Party aide, Wesley McCune. Its modern equivalent is the Media Matters group.

The Kennedy and Johnson Administrations saw the Fairness Doctrine as a useful and effective tool to silence opponents of the liberal agenda and "provide support for the President's programs" and other "high-priority legislation," Friendly notes. One such campaign was launched in support of the Nuclear Test Ban Treaty, using a bipartisan front organization organized by the Democratic National Committee and backed by the White House. Arthur Larson, one of those involved in the campaign, is quoted by Friendly as saying that "...we decided to use the Fairness Doctrine to harass the extreme right. In the light of Watergate, it was wrong. We felt the ends justified the means. They never do." In the end, the campaign had produced 1,035 letters to stations, producing a total of 1,678 hours of free time from stations carrying conservative media personalities.

The "Hate Clubs of the Air" article explained how the campaign would proceed, advising liberals to "demand free time to counter some of the radical right's wild-swinging charges." Victor Lasky explained that "These demands for equal time, which stations would have to provide gratis, were regarded by most of their executives as harassments they'd rather avoid. Thus many of them did, either by dropping the commentaries or by censoring them."

We can expect the same modus operandi under a new Fairness Doctrine.

Once dubbed the "Hush Rush" bill, the new version of the Fairness Doctrine would actually go far beyond Rush Limbaugh and target hundreds of conservative talk show hosts on the local, regional and national levels. Sean Hannity, Laura Ingraham, Michael Savage and TV personalities such as Bill O'Reilly and Neil Cavuto could be forced by federal bureaucrats to turn over part of their programs to liberals and left-wingers who disagree with them. If they refuse, their stations or companies could be fined by the FCC, their broadcasting licenses threatened or revoked, and the shows even taken off the air. This plan is also a direct threat to the Christian radio and TV broadcasters who present a conservative or Christian message to the American people.

Don't think it can't happen here, because this is the plan that was laid out at the "National Conference on Media Reform." In addition to Sen. Sanders and Rep. Hinchey, speakers at the event included Bill Moyers of public TV, Jesse Jackson, and Hollywood celebrities such as Jane Fonda.

The talking points of the new left-wing censors have already filtered down to the grass roots. One activist on the liberal website www. bluesunbelt.com declared:

"We can pass legislation that will restore local media ownership, the Fairness Doctrine and Equal Time Protection in broadcasting and demand the return of anti-monopoly regulations for all media outlets.

"Democrats can start publishing local community newsletters. We can organize Letter to the Editor campaigns and talk radio call-in campaigns in every community. Democrats should complain to radio stations, TV stations and newspapers about unfair articles, stories and editorials. Demand balance. If you have to petition or picket a media outlet, do it and contact competitors to publicize your efforts. Seek allies from the union movement and reform organizations."

THE COVER-UP

The deep involvement of the Kennedy and Johnson Administrations in the organized assault on the conservative media wasn't disclosed until Fred W. Friendly wrote his 1975 book, examining the background to and circumstances surrounding the Supreme Court's 1969 Red Lion decision upholding the federal Fairness Doctrine. As Victor Lasky notes, Friendly disclosed that the decision was "tainted" in that the Supreme Court was unaware that the case resulted from a White House effort to suppress conservative voices in the media.

In the Red Lion case, Fred Cook, a liberal author and contributor to The Nation magazine, claimed that a Philadelphia radio station, WGCB, had unfairly attacked him by airing a commentary from a conservative preacher. The FCC was asked to intervene and ordered the station to give Cook free reply time under the Fairness Doctrine. The station's owner, Red Lion Broadcasting Company, refused, and the case went to court. As Lasky notes, this ruling upheld the right of the FCC "to order a broadcaster to grant reply time to a person or group claiming to have suffered from a broadcast." The Fairness Doctrine was abolished under the Reagan Administration.

But because the abolition of the Fairness Doctrine led to the expansion of talk radio, featuring conservative voices, the "progressives" have been trying to figure out a way to bring it back. The advent of cable news, whose most popular channel, Fox News, includes conservative voices, has only added to liberal frustration with the "new media."

Hinchey, in his remarks to the Media Reform conference, said the survival of America was itself at stake because "neo-fascist" and "neo-con" talk-show hosts led by Rush Limbaugh had facilitated the "illegal" war in Iraq and were complicit in President Bush's repeated violations of the Constitution, such as by detaining terrorists. He warned that the "right-wing oriented media" were now preparing the way for Bush to wage war on Iran and Syria.

CONGRESSIONAL ACTION

His answer, a bill titled the "Media Ownership Reform Act," would reinstate the Fairness Doctrine and authorize bureaucrats at the FCC to monitor and alter the content of radio and television programs. With passage of his bill, Hinchey said that "progressives" would be able to demand and get "equal access" to programs hosted by conservatives and rebut the "baloney" of people like Limbaugh. "All of that stuff will end," Hinchey said about the influence of conservative media. By name, he also denounced Fox News and Sinclair Broadcasting.

The Hinchey bill was cosponsored by 16 legislators in the last session of Congress. All of them were Democrats except for independent Rep. Bernard Sanders, who was subsequently elected as an independent Senator from Vermont: Reps. Peter A. DeFazio (Or.), Bob Filner (Ca.), Alcee Hastings (Fl.), Marcy Kaptur (Oh.), Barbara Lee (Ca.), Jim McDermott (Wa.), James P. Moran (Va.), Major Owens (NY.), Janice Schakowsky (Il.), Louise Slaughter (NY.), Hilda L. Solis (Ca.), Fortney Stark

(Ca.), Maxine Waters (Ca.), Diane Watson (Ca.), and Lynn C. Woolsey (Ca.).

Slaughter had her own Fairness and Accountability in Broadcasting Act. Its cosponsors were all Democrats except for independent socialist Rep. Bernard Sanders.

On January 26, 2005, Slaughter had hosted a panel on the subject of "Should the Congress reinstitute media standards through the creation of a Media and Fairness in Broadcasting Act?" The panel included Mark Lloyd, Senior Fellow, Center for American Progress; David Brock of Media Matters; Gloria Tristani, former FCC Commissioner, Chellie Pingree, President and CEO, Common Cause; Tom Athans of Democracy Radio; and Sam Seder, Co-host of Air America's Majority Report.

Accuracy in Media anticipates that the push for the Fairness Doctrine will include stacked hearings before various Democratic-controlled congressional committees or subcommittees. These include the House Subcommittee on Telecommunications and the Internet, chaired by Rep. Edward Markey (Mass.). However, Rep. Dennis Kucinich (D-Oh.), has announced that he will hold hearings on restoring the Fairness Doctrine through the Domestic Policy Subcommittee of the Government Reform Committee. Kucinich, chair of the subcommittee, claims his jurisdiction includes telecommunications and that he will have oversight over the FCC.

Interestingly, Kucinich has not succumbed to the "progressive" campaign to boycott Fox News. The Fox News Channel, he says, "is a legitimate news agency that has the ability to reach out to millions of Americans..." He says that liberals and Democrats have to be able to "stand the scrutiny" of the channel and be able to go toe-to-toe with its news anchors. That is part of the test of leadership, he says.

But leadership, in his view, also involves bringing back the Fairness Doctrine. "We are now in a position to move a progressive agenda to where it is visible," he says.

V

Hate Radio:
Oklahoma City and Beyond

By Lynn Woolley

President Bill Clinton never mentioned Rush Limbaugh by name during his speech in Minneapolis. But he left little doubt that "El Rushbo" was on his mind as he discussed the underlying causes that led to the bombing of the Alfred P. Murrah Federal Building in Oklahoma City:

Clinton said the nation's airwaves are too often used "to keep some people as paranoid as possible and the rest of us upset with each other. [Such people] spread hate, they leave the impression that, by their very words, that violence is acceptable... It is time we all stood up and spoke against that kind of reckless speech and behavior."

By implication, the President of the United States was saying that while Timothy McVeigh may have set off the bomb, it was really right-wing talk radio, led by Rush Limbaugh, that created the climate for such hatred.

The Left has come to call it "Hate Radio."

The Media Research Center in Washington called Clinton's bluff and offered $100,000 to anyone who could cite a conservative talk host who was inciting this type of behavior. Someone brought up G. Gordon Liddy's comments about what to do if a government agent comes

43

to your house to take your guns away. But that was the best the Left could do.

Still, Clinton had drawn a line in the sand. If the Left can't neuter a conservative talk show using the "fairness" argument, it will attempt to brand a host as a "hater" and throw him off the air entirely. The fact of the matter is that the Left has spilled almost as much ink on the subject of "Hate Radio"—a term they cherish dearly—as they have on the more nebulous concept of "balance." After all, if the idea of the Fairness Doctrine as "fair and balanced" is successfully utilized, Rush Limbaugh may very well remain on the air. But brand him as a purveyor of Hate Radio, and, like Don Imus, he could be removed completely.

In the aftermath of Mr. Clinton's speech—which, naturally, was the subject of many a Limbaugh monologue and even a column in Newsweek entitled "Why I'm Not to Blame"—presidential aides hastened to point out that he never mentioned the name "Rush Limbaugh."

But, as William F. Buckley, Jr. wrote in National Review on May 29, 1995: "…who did he have in mind? Unless the person doing all those things on the airwaves is a pretty big fixture on the national scene, surely the President of the United States would not bother to single him out for national attention? If it was somebody who got on the air from Tuscaloosa one night to empty his bile, that wouldn't quality as the object of the President's attention. Right?"

Exactly right.

Clinton was, in fact, doing what he was accusing Limbaugh of doing. The thought process on the Left goes something like this: Mr. Limbaugh and his ilk are constantly raving about "Big Government" and how it has become involved in too much of our lives. To the Left, this is nonsense since Big Government is a goal, but never mind that. Rush is keeping up the pressure day after day, raising the stakes, demonizing Big Government, and you know what? There are crazies out there that are soaking it all in. You know the type—gun nuts, pro-lifers, the Religious Right. With all this Hate Radio, doesn't it make sense that some of them might snap? After all, isn't Rush suggesting between the lines that violence is all right if it's directed at evil Big Government?

Of course, by deflecting the blame to conservative talk radio, President Clinton was able to smear his political enemies and, at the same time, deflect any blame for the event from his own administration.

FAIR GOES ON THE ATTACK

As reported by Ralph R. Reiland in Insight On the News, August 12, 2002, other liberals picked up on Clinton's rhetoric and even expanded it to cover most on the Right:

"Falling into line, columnist Carl Rowan wrote that he was 'absolutely certain' that 'the harsher rhetoric of the Gingriches and the Doles creates a climate of violence in America.' Timothy McVeigh... was, in Rowan's words, a 'triggerman' for Republicans. Added Bryant Gumbel: 'The bombing in Oklahoma City has focused renewed attention on the rhetoric that's been coming from the Right and those who cater to angry white men.'"

Liberal watchdog groups like "Fairness and Accuracy In Reporting" (FAIR) weighed in on the Oklahoma City controversy as well, accusing conservative talk radio of jumping to conclusions. This quote is from Jim Naureckas in his article "Talk Radio on Oklahoma City: Don't look at us" from Extra! July/August, 1995: "...it seemed to us that most talk radio in the days immediately after the blast was even more reckless and extreme than TV journalists in its rush to blame Muslims."

FAIR pulled some out-of-context quotes to bolster its attack:

"You know why these Middle Eastern terrorists chose Oklahoma City?" said an unnamed Chicago host cited in the Chicago Sun-Times of April 24, 1995. "Because it's in the heartland of America, and if they can strike there, they can strike anywhere."

From WRKO/Boston's Howie Carr on April 20, 1995: "What are we going to do with these towelheads?"

FAIR even reported that, on the very same day, WABC/New York's Bob Grant discussed the possibility of actually killing a guest who didn't buy his argument that Muslims were to blame: "What I'd like to do is put you against the wall with the rest of them, and mow you down with them."

To FAIR, these extreme examples of unfairly blaming innocent

Muslims are proof that Bill Clinton was right. From the Naureckas piece: "Such rhetoric seems to vindicate President Bill Clinton's charge that there are 'purveyors of hate and division' on U.S. airwaves who 'leave the impression, by their very words, that violence is acceptable.' Clinton was roundly condemned by right-wing talk radio hosts and their allies for 'politicizing' the Oklahoma City bombing, but his basic point is undeniable: There is much speech on the radio today that advocates or justifies violence."

Whether you agree with Grant or not, it's quite a stretch to place blame on talk radio for the idea that radical Muslims might have been involved in the Oklahoma City bombing. Soon after the incident took place, there had been an all-points bulletin issued by the Oklahoma City Police alerting law enforcement officers to be on the lookout for "a late-model Chevrolet full-size pickup, brown in color, with tinted windows." According to the APB, the truck was occupied by "two Middle Eastern males, 25 to 28 years of age, six feet tall, athletic build, dark hair and a beard."

Some journalists still insist that there is a Middle Eastern connection. Chief among them is Oklahoma City television reporter Jayna Davis, who wrote in her book *The Third Terrorist,* about the still-unexplained abandonment of the search for "John Doe #2" whom she believes was a part of Saddam Hussein's elite Republican Guard.

Indeed, the preponderance of mainstream reporting in the immediate wake of the explosion centered on a Middle Eastern connection; it wasn't solely talk radio. And in the wake of the attacks of September 11, 2001, it's quite clear that anyone who didn't consider the possibility of Middle Eastern terrorists in OKC might have been a bit naïve.

But of course, the Oklahoma City bombing is not the only instance in which the left has waved an accusing finger—and we won't mention which finger—at talk radio.

ON THE LIBERAL RADAR

Lowell Ponte, writing in the June, 2007 issue of *NewsMax Magazine,* discusses who might be next on the Left's list of targets following the Don Imus affair. He mentions a slew of hosts who are on the radar of the liberal watchdog group Media Matters for America:

- Glenn Beck for calling Rosie O'Donnell a "fat witch."
- WSB/Atlanta syndicated host Neil Boortz for saying that in a national disaster, "we should save the rich people first. They are the ones that are responsible for this prosperity."
- Rush for opining that some women "would love to be hired as eye candy."
- Michael Savage for saying that the average prostitute is more reliable and more honest than most U.S. senators.
- Fox News Channel's and Westwood One's Bill O'Reilly for his agreeing with a caller that illegal immigrants "bring corrupting influences" and "a Third World value system" to America.
- Fox's John Gibson for his report that nearly half the children in the United States 5 or younger are Hispanic, and for telling viewers to "do your duty—make more babies…Hispanics can't carry the whole load."
- WPHT/Philadelphia host Michael Smerconish for saying that political correctness has made the United States "a nation of sissies."

Again, we don't have the context for these comments, but it's obvious that several of them are satire—something the humor-challenged Left doesn't understand. Boortz's comment is satire with a touch of truth, Limbaugh's is almost certainly true, and Gibson's makes a valid point while being hilarious at the same time. To the Left, these comments constitute Hate Radio and are grounds for throwing these hate-monger hosts off the air!

THE G-MAN CONTROVERSY

Absent from this list, but at the top of many earlier lists is the Watergate figure G. Gordon Liddy who parlayed his fame into a talk radio career, and for a while, was one of the top three hosts in the country.

"The most notorious practitioner of Hate Radio today is G. Gordon Liddy, whose instructions about shooting federal agents in the head seemed to epitomize the kind of speech Clinton confirmed," gushed FAIR's Naureckas. "Liddy, a convicted Watergate felon who is heard on some 250 stations, likes to give the impression that he speaks for an armed movement that is ready to use its extensive weaponry against government forces."

Once again, the quote is wildly out of context. Here's the text of what Liddy said on his show of August 26, 1994:

> "Now if the Bureau of Alcohol, Tobacco and Firearms
> comes to disarm you and they are bearing arms, resist them
> with arms. Go for a head shot; they're going to be wearing
> bulletproof vests... They've got a big target on there, ATF.
> Don't shoot at that, because they've got a vest on under-
> neath that. Head shots, head shots. Kill the sons of bitches."

Liddy, who won the "Freedom of Speech Award" at Michael Harrison's talk radio convention in Houston in 1995 based on this comment, answers his critics in an online interview with John Hawkins:

> "I was talking about a situation in which the Bureau of Al-
> cohol, Tobacco and Firearms comes smashing into a house,
> doesn't say who they are, and their guns are out, they're
> shooting, and they're in the wrong place. This has happened
> time and time again. The ATF has gone in and gotten the
> wrong guy in the wrong place. The law is that if somebody
> is shooting at you, using deadly force, the mere fact that
> they are a law enforcement officer, if they are in the wrong,
> does not mean you are obliged to allow yourself to be killed
> so your kinfolk can have a wrongful death action. You are
> legally entitled to defend yourself and I was speaking of
> exactly those kind of situations. If you're going to do that,
> you should know that they're wearing body armor so you
> should use a head shot. Now all I'm doing is stating the law,
> but all the nuances in there got left out when the story got
> repeated."

It's interesting to note at this point that Liddy isn't on the radar screens quite so much since the ascendancy of so many of his peers on the Right. That is to say, there are bigger targets such as those mentioned by Media Matters. But the biggest prize of all remains the Doctor of Democracy. The liberals would seemingly pay any price to bring down Rush Limbaugh.

BRING ME THE HEAD OF RUSH LIMBAUGH

Just as Mr. Liddy has been saddled with the ATF comments, so has El Rushbo been tarnished with the stain of a passing comment made ubiquitous by the Left. Some of them even keep video copies for duplicating and mail-out purposes; your writer knows this because a liberal friend made sure to send one.

We speak, of course, of the infamous Chelsea Clinton as "the White House Dog" comment from the Rush Limbaugh syndicated television show.

As the liberals tell it, here's what happened:

"On his TV show, early in the Clinton administration, Limbaugh put up a picture of Socks, the White House cat, and asked, 'Did you know there's a White House dog?' Then, he put up a picture of Chelsea Clinton, who was 13 years old at the time and as far as I know had never done any harm to anyone."

This is from the late Texas progressive Molly Ivins who rejected Mr. Limbaugh's assertion that the on-air bit was an accident—that someone in the control booth had put up the photo without his permission. Having viewed the offending piece, it's hard to say what the truth is. It could have been an out-of-control video tech. But the routine had to be going somewhere. Maybe a photo of Hillary Clinton was the original plan. In any case, this was a tasteless attempt at humor —nothing more—and Rush learned from it and thereafter refrained from making Chelsea a part of his commentary.

If an underage and nonpolitical child rightly should be off limits to satire—how about a serving member of an administration? Nope; to Molly Ivins, even Rush's bits on the stature of then-Labor Secretary Robert W. Reich constituted Hate Radio as she wrote in *Mother Jones,* May/June, 1995:

"Limbaugh put up a picture of [Reich] that showed him from the forehead up, as though that was all the camera could get. Reich is indeed a very short man as a result of a bone disease he had as a child. Somehow, the effect of bone disease in children has never struck me as an appropriate topic for humor." One is left to wonder what does strike liberals as topics for appropriate humor? She never mentioned it in her Mother Jones piece, but Molly might have chuckled at the title and contents of Al Franken's book *Rush Limbaugh is a Big Fat Idiot,* or, perhaps she giggled at MSNBC's Keith Olbermann's constant bashing of Bill O'Reilly on his "Worst Person in the World" segments. She might have enjoyed editorial cartoons that caricature the facial features of people like George W. Bush in order to make them seem ridiculous.

The fact is, that political parody is a time-honored tradition in this country, and sometimes it's really funny. The Left only chortles when the satire is aimed at those on the Right. Presumably, when Mr. Franken does it, it's parody. When Rush does it, it's Hate Radio.

OBAMA THE MAGIC NEGRO

This begs the question: Can the Left actually use the charge of Hate Radio to toss conservative hosts off the air, or even to have them charged with hate crimes? Don't think for a minute they won't try.

On March 19, 2007, David Ehrenstein wrote a column in the Los Angeles Times referring to Barack Obama as "The Magic Negro."

Ehrenstein wrote about the mythical "Magic Negro" as a figure of folk culture to explain a black person who appears, seemingly out of nowhere, to help whites with their guilt:

"He's there to assuage white 'guilt' (i.e. the minimal discomfort they feel) over the role of slavery and racial segregation in American history, while replacing stereotypes of a dangerous, highly sexualized black man with a benign figure for whom interracial sexual congress holds no interest."

If you read that and exclaimed "huh?" you're likely not alone. Ehrenstein, who is black, presumably wrote it to explain the popularity of Obama among some whites. But whether the column was brilliant insight or progressive psychobabble, it was just the type of thing Rush Limbaugh would seize upon for comedy relief. And it didn't take him long!

You might be thinking—wait a minute! Why would Rush do this in the wake of the now-infamous Donovan McNabb incident in 2003 in which Mr. Limbaugh said on ESPN that the Eagles quarterback wasn't talented and received attention because the media wanted a black to do well.

The answer to that is not likely as complicated as liberal think tanks might have you believe. Probably, Rush saw the opportunity for a funny bit that would poke fun at a bunch of liberal institutions at the same time including the LA Times, Obama, Peter, Paul & Mary, the Rev. Al Sharpton, and of course, the silly notion of the Magic Negro.

The concept was a natural: Use the article and the term to rewrite Peter Yarrow's 1963 song "Puff the Magic Dragon" and make it a parody. Since the Magic Negro concept involves the issue of black authenticity, the parody had Paul Shanklin, as Sharpton, calling out Obama as being "not authentic like me."

It was insensitive by design. But it made its point: the civil rights Reverend (at least in the parody) was not happy that a Magic Negro has come along to supplant him as one of the two titular heads of the black political community. The obligatory outcries of racism hit a fever pitch with this op-ed headline in the May 17, 2007 edition of the Houston Chronicle.

"Is Limbaugh above the law?"

From the title, you'd think that writer Andrew Guy, Jr. was about to list the statutes that Mr. Limbaugh had apparently violated. Instead, the article was simply a rant, pointing out that both Limbaugh and Shanklin are white (a non sequitur if ever there was one) and asking, "Is Limbaugh getting a free pass?"

Guy lamented the fact that while Don Imus had been fired for calling a group of basketball players "nappy headed hos" Limbaugh was getting off scot-free.

Guy should refer to his Constitution and court cases that unambiguously preserve the right to freedom of speech and particularly to political parody. The Rutgers lady basketball team was not running for office nor had it injected its way in any form into current events. But everyone and every institution that got skewered in the Shanklin parody was intimately involved in politics.

Mr. Guy's column was all emotion, but such is the state of opinion on the Left. If anyone is fired over this piece, perhaps it should be the Chronicle's headline writer. As a writer on the newspaper's blog noted:

"So when did the Chronicle's editors determine that 'airing the works' of somebody else (so long as the proper permissions were obtained) is ILLEGAL? Just curious. Is it a misdemeanor, or a felony, eh? What is the penalty? Can you cite the statute that is being violated?"

Obviously, no laws were broken by Mr. Limbaugh, Mr. Shanklin, or even by Mr. Guy who is free to write emotion-based nonsense if he wants to. The Magic Negro parody may have turned some heads on the Left, but most realized that it wasn't the smoking gun they'd been hoping for.

And they ARE hoping.

COUNTDOWN TO CENSORSHIP

MSNBC's rising star of the Left, Keith Olbermann, openly calls Limbaugh "racist." He demands to know why none of the "racist right" have been fired as Imus was. Under Ditto-Cam footage of Rush Limbaugh the "Countdown" screen displays the graphic "Selective Outrage."

This was taking place on April 12, some days after Limbaugh had offended Mr. Olbermann by referring to Barack Obama as "Halfrican American." Actually, that description is clever for two reasons: First, Mr. Obama is the offspring of a white mother and a black father. Second, it is another parody of liberals who insist on classifying everyone by race. But never mind that—Olbermann was offended and it's not nice to offend liberals. So Olbermann and his guest, Air America's Sam Seder, were busy offending conservatives, which is all right.

The conversation went this way:

OLBERMANN: "I'll ask you the ten million dollar question: How does Rush Limbaugh or Michael Savage get away with worse than what Don Imus said?"
SEDER: "I'll tell you something, well I think one there's a certain expectation that they're going to hear it more from

Limbaugh although, you know, he, Dick Cheney was on his program several weeks ago. I listened in to Limbaugh today and he's already warning his audience that they're going to be coming for Limbaugh next. And I think, frankly, he's got to be a little bit worried now because the bar has just been raised.

I mean, corporations have said we're not going to tolerate this any more and the next time Limbaugh slips up, which I think is inevitable, I think you're going to see this sort of same type of reaction."

OLBERMANN: "It's the best thing I've heard in a couple of days."

SEDER, over Olbermann: "I hope so."

OLBERMANN: "From your lips to God's ears!"

Frankly, we doubt that Rush Limbaugh is "worried" over comments made on an all-liberal platform like "Countdown with Keith Olbermann"—a show that features virtually no opposing viewpoints. But Rush, like all other conservatives hosts, is vigilant.

He knows that it wasn't the issue of balance that cost Don Imus his job. It was the charge of "insensitivity" blown up by the Left to its most extreme form.

Just imagine if today's spate of hate-crimes legislation could be construed by liberal judges to encompass talk radio. Already, the state can prosecute people for their "feelings" of animosity toward certain protected classes including crimes involving race, religion, ethnicity and national origin. It's quite possible that other classes might be added to the list including gender, sexual orientation and disability. It's not much of a stretch that a liberal administration coupled with a willing Congress might make it a hate crime to bring up such issues over the airwaves.

It could be nothing more than a slip of the tongue, an off-hand comment, or biting political parody. It might be an outright mistake on the part of some overzealous host. No matter; the Left will characterize it as Hate Radio, and along with the return of the Fairness Doctrine, it's the biggest threat to freedom of speech over the air.

VI

THE INSIDE STORY OF THE DON IMUS AFFAIR

BY CLIFF KINCAID

D
o you think something was fishy about the Don Imus affair? Why was the boom lowered on him at that time? The answer may have something to do with his main accuser, the Media Matters group, which is emerging as a front organization for Senator Hillary Clinton's presidential campaign and has extensive ties to the national Democratic Party. In firing Imus, NBC News and CBS got rid of one of Hillary's major political enemies in the media. The campaign against Imus should be seen as a trial run for how the Fairness Doctrine might work in practice.

Glenn Thrush of Newsday wrote a revealing September 7, 2006, article about the relationship between Senator Clinton and David Brock, the former conservative who runs Media Matters. Calling it the "Clinton-Brock alliance," Thrush revealed that Hillary "advised Brock on creating the group" and "chats with him occasionally and thinks he provides a valuable service…" Thrush added, "For her part, Clinton's extended family of contributors, consultants and friends has played a pivotal role in helping Media Matters grow from a $3.5 million start-up in 2004 to its current $8.5 million budget."

Another key funding source for Media Matters (and much of the left-wing movement in this country) is George Soros, the billionaire financial speculator who profits at the expense and decay of Western civilization. His causes include legalization of marijuana and other drugs, gun control, abortion rights, gay rights, rights for felons, opposition to the death penalty, rights for illegal immigrants, and euthanasia. On foreign affairs, Soros, a big backer of the United Nations, is associated with opposition to the U.S. policy of resisting the rise of radical and anti-American Islamic groups and states. He spent $26 million in 2004 trying to defeat President Bush.

Media Matters claims that it does not receive money from Soros directly or indirectly through the Democracy Alliance, a group of wealthy "progressive" donors, including Soros, that was the subject of rumors in the left-wing press that it was a front group for Hillary's 2008 presidential campaign. However, Media Matters has been publicly identified (and confirmed by Democracy Alliance founder Rob Stein) as an organization that "we have funded."

THE "INSIDE STORY"

By now, everyone knows the basic story of Don Imus. A shock jock who had been saying shocking things on his radio/TV show for years, said some more shocking things and got fired. But why was he singled out for firing after all these years of saying shocking things? Some are saying that it had something to do with his latest victims, the mostly black Rutgers women's basketball team. The rationale is that insulting this particular group of people was somehow over the line, as compared with all of his other jokes, insults and putdowns. But that argument isn't very convincing. There is something else to this story.

In a Dateline NBC report by correspondent Dennis Murphy, we are being given the official "inside story" of Imus's firing. Murphy briefly alludes to the role of the "liberal watchdog group," Media Matters, in the controversy, and claims that various NBC News employees played a key role in getting Imus fired. But Murphy's corporate line has to be dismissed completely out of hand because of his ridiculous assertion that Al Sharpton, a notorious racial demagogue, was merely a "civil rights leader" who played a big role in the affair. If Murphy won't or can't tell the truth about Sharpton's sordid background, you know he's not leveling with his audience about what really happened inside NBC.

Asked by Murphy if the network was caving in to pressure groups, NBC News President Steven Capus replied that, "Rather than portraying it as caving to pressure groups, I would say that we listened to America." Capus must believe we are all saps.

PROTECTING HILLARY

The real "inside story," as Newsday's Thrush indicated, is that Media Matters, the organization that initially taped and distributed Imus's racist remarks about the Rutgers basketball team, has extremely close ties to Hillary. Media Matters had been after Imus for months because of his treatment of Hillary, noting as far back as May 2006 that he had referred to her as "Satan" and a "witch." Media Matters called this attempted humor a "smear" and urged its followers to contact MSNBC and "take action" and protest.

It didn't matter that Imus specialized in insults that were laughed at or dismissed by most people, including his victims. In the Media Matters world, where Hillary rules, you are not supposed to say anything seriously or comically critical of the former First Lady.

While NBC News is claiming that black news personnel played a critical role in getting Imus fired, and that network executives responded to them with interest and sensitivity, it was a white liberal, Keith Olbermann, who boasted on his own MSNBC "Countdown" show on April 11, 2007, that he told his bosses "behind the scenes" that a decision to remove Imus "had to be made." Olbermann is a Clinton sycophant who specializes in attacking others who are perceived to be too tough on the Clintons, both Bill and Hillary, and other Democrats. But he has some leverage at the network, based on having recently signed a new four-year contract.

THE NEW TARGETS

It was during this program, while interviewing Jesse Jackson, that Olbermann provided a new list of targets. He told Jackson that "Don Imus was not alone among those who have made remarks like this, let me go through a few names and then ask you a question in terms of momentum, in terms of fairness." He then cited:

> "Comments by people like Rush Limbaugh, who calls Sena-
> tor Barack Obama and actress Halle Berry, quote, 'halfrican-
> Americans.' Michael Savage, who asked whether the Voting
> Right Acts intended to counteract racial discrimination at
> the ballot box was trying to, quote, 'put a chad in every crack
> house.' There's Neil Boortz, the other radio talker, who said
> the black congressman Cynthia McKinney looked, quote,
> 'like a ghetto slut.' Glenn Beck from CNN and ABC, who
> referred to the largely African-American survivors of Hurri-
> cane Katrina in New Orleans as, quote, 'scumbags,' and who,
> when he interviewed the Black Muslim congressman, Keith
> Ellison, from Minnesota, said he felt like saying to him, 'Sir,
> prove to me that you are not working with our enemies.'
> Where is the protest, where have you been, why are there
> not efforts to remove them from the air for these things?"

In response, Jackson agreed that "The air is toxic," and said that
"The momentum to detoxify the airwaves to create a higher decency
standard for our children, must apply across the board."

The same day, April 11, Al Franken, who is running for the Senate
in Minnesota as a Democrat, was on CNN's Larry King Live, endorsing
the firing of Imus and asking CNN to fire Glenn Beck for questioning
the loyalty to the U.S. of Muslim Rep. Keith Ellison. Franken went on
to say, "And I hear this kind of thing a lot of time. I monitored a lot
of right-wing radio when I was doing my show and before it. And I've
heard Rush Limbaugh say things that are worse than this."

The next day, Media Matters was out with a list of targets and
alleged bigoted and sexist quotes, citing the names on Olbermann's
list and adding Ann Coulter and Tucker Carlson, now on MSNBC.
The Free Press, the George Soros-funded group behind the "National
Conference on Media Reform," issued an "action alert" declaring that
"getting rid of Imus won't fix the media problem," that Imus was "just
the tip of the iceberg," and that "Scores of other TV and radio hosts
regularly make racist and sexist comments." The liberal Huffington

Post website followed with a front page that accused O'Reilly and Limbaugh of making disparaging comments about minorities.

O'Reilly was so concerned about the charge, based on his on-air reference to "Mexican wetbacks" during a discussion of illegal immigration, that he brought Howard Kurtz of the Washington Post on his radio show to agree that it was not a racist comment. O'Reilly said he had "misspoke" and that he meant to use the word "coyotes." Kurtz said, "I did not think that you were deliberately trying to insult the Mexican people, if that's what you're asking." O'Reilly replied, "Thank you for your honesty." O'Reilly played this exchange on his TV show.

Kurtz, who had been a guest on the Imus show, offers the Fox News Channel host a sense of protection from the Media Matters group, often labeled by O'Reilly as a "smear site" that wants "to silence me."

Another left-wing media watchdog group, Fairness & Accuracy in Reporting (FAIR), published a report insisting that O'Reilly had a history of making racial slurs. Such attacks may help explain why O'Reilly, on the evening of April 18, paid homage to Al Sharpton at his National Action Network Convention. O'Reilly must calculate that the only way to avoid the Imus treatment is to buy protection from the "Reverend."

MOUTHPIECE FOR THE CENSORS

It is highly ironic, however, that Olbermann, who smears people by labeling them as "The Worst" in the world on a nightly basis, should stay on the air in the wake of the Imus firing. I was labeled a "Worst Person in the World" for drawing attention to Democratic Senator and presidential candidate Joseph Biden's racist comments about Senator Barack Obama. In attacking me, Olbermann falsely claimed that Bush had made similar remarks. The former sportscaster can claim he's just joking when he identifies someone as "The Worst Person in the World," but Imus said that he was joking, too. Olbermann's approach is mean-spirited, amateurish and beneath the dignity of a serious news operation.

Not surprisingly, Media Matters has a direct pipeline into Olbermann's program. Media Matters President and CEO David Brock has appeared on Olbermann's show, and Olbermann makes use of Media Matters material. Media Matters, in turn, highlights his attacks on conservatives.

But you don't have to be a conservative to come under attack by the Olbermann/Media Matters axis. A recent and amusing example is their coordinated attack on Karen Tumulty of Time magazine for writing a piece about Hillary's political exploitation of the Imus controversy. For daring to suggest that the former First Lady might be using the incident for fundraising purposes, Tumulty was given a "bronze" medal in the "Worst Person in the World" segment.

The working relationship between Olbermann and this left-wing pressure group not only puts in question the "independence" of MSN-BC in the Imus matter but the ability of Olbermann and his producers to come up with original and fresh material. Of course, NBC News correspondent Dennis Murphy didn't mention any of this in his "inside story" about Imus's downfall. What a convenient and interesting omission.

A TROUBLED CHILDHOOD

Brock's 2002 book, *Blinded by the Right,* is quite extraordinary in that it begins with a prologue admitting that the author was responsible for telling "lies" and ruining reputations. Assuming some parts of the book are true, at least those concerning Brock personally, it describes a young man struggling with an immoral lifestyle. Writing about college, for example, he says, "With some hesitation, during my freshman year, I went on uneasy dates and had hurried sexual encounters with other guys in neighboring dorms." Later, he writes that he would go "out to bars looking for one-night hookups with some frequency, always by myself, very late at night, with few knowing, and no one caring, who I was."

Today, out of the closet and a certified "progressive" activist with money from the Clinton machine and other big-name liberals, some people know of Brock because his group has emerged as the moral arbiter, along with Al Sharpton, of what should or should not be said on the airwaves. It would be laughable were it not so serious for the future of freedom of speech and broadcasting in this country.

In fact, some of the Media Matters complaints about the media are comical. It once urged people to protest when Bill O'Reilly of Fox News reportedly said that he wished that Hurricane Katrina had flooded the United Nations building in New York "and I wouldn't have rescued them." This joke was denounced as "hate speech" by Brock, who said that the comment "does not belong on America's airwaves" and is "wrong and un-American." Media Matters called attention to a letter from Tim Wirth, head of the Ted Turner-financed U.N. Foundation, who called for a "public apology" from O'Reilly.

But if the problem was merely that Media Matters simply had no sense of humor, the organization itself could be dismissed with a laugh. Instead, however, it has a big problem with truth-telling and follows in Brock's footsteps by trying to ruin people and reputations.

My only encounter with Brock came when he was a conservative and wanted help with an article he was writing about the left-wing Christic Institute. I had researched the organization extensively and had debated its leader on C-SPAN. I provided much of my research to Brock, who came into my office, on the condition that he credit me in his piece. He did not. I learned then that he could not be trusted.

Years later, when he became an ex-conservative, his Media Matters group published an item falsely implying that I had fabricated a letter from the Afghan Ambassador. The Brock group rushed into print with this defamatory item without checking the facts beforehand. Then it refused to retract or apologize after being caught. Like Brock, the organization can't be trusted to say or do what is right.

THE SOROS CONNECTION

In the same vein, the organization tries to mislead and confuse people about its connection to George Soros, the left-wing billionaire convicted of inside trading in France who finances the ACLU, the Drug Policy Alliance, and other such groups. Although Media Matters receives funding from the so-called Democracy Alliance, which is funded by George Soros, it also claims that it has "never received funding" from him. Since the Democracy Alliance does not publish a list of its members or a list of the organizations it funds, this claim cannot be accepted at face value. We know that Soros has been acknowledged to be a member of the Democracy Alliance and that its founder Rob Stein acknowledges providing funds to Media Matters. Most importantly, Media Matters defends Soros, describing him merely as a "progressive philanthropist," about as frequently as it defends Hillary.

The funding of Media Matters through the Democracy Alliance adds another layer of media protection for the controversial billionaire, as AIM has documented in a special report how he has put millions of dollars into "investigative reporting" and news organizations. Such payments guarantee that the news groups won't target Soros for scrutiny.

Prominent members of the Democracy Alliance, in addition to Soros, include insurance magnate Peter Lewis, another supporter of drug legalization who was arrested in New Zealand several years ago after customs officers found marijuana in his luggage. The Democracy Alliance was started by Rob Stein, a former Clinton official.

Demonstrating the sensitivity of receiving money from Soros, Media Matters admits receiving money from "donors" to the Democracy Alliance but claims, in the face of the evidence about how the organization is run, that it doesn't take any money from Soros himself. This is an untenable and false position to assert, as published reports about the organization in the Washington Post and even The Nation have never indicated that Soros money has been segregated so as not to go to certain groups like Media Matters.

LINKS TO THE DEMOCRATIC PARTY

The connections of Media Matters to the Democratic Party are also substantial, suggesting that the organization functions largely as a Democratic Party front. The group's "senior adviser," Dennis Yedwab, served as the director of strategic resources at the Democratic Congressional Campaign Committee and research director at the Democratic Senatorial Campaign Committee. Other staffers have come from the Al Gore campaign, the Clinton-Gore 1996 Committee, the ACLU, the Gay & Lesbian Victory Fund, and the Soros-funded Center for American Progress (which also gave Media Matters some office space when it was being formed). John Podesta, president and CEO of the Center for American Progress, served as Chief of Staff to President

Clinton from October 1998 until January 2001.

Katie Barge, the former director of research for Media Matters, became research director for the Democratic Senatorial Campaign Committee (DSCC), only to resign under fire when she was alleged to have participated in an effort to fraudulently obtain a credit report on Maryland's Republican Lt. Gov. Michael S. Steele, who was running for the U.S. Senate. Her subordinate at the DSCC, Lauren B. Weiner, was charged with a crime in the case but there was no explanation of why Barge was not. Barge is now a spokesperson for a left-wing Christian group opposed to the Iraq war and director of communications strategy for a religious left organization known as Faith in Public Life. Her official bio carefully omits any mention of her role in the scandal involving Steele's credit report.

As we point out in our special report, "Left-wing Censorship Campaign Targets Conservative Media," Media Matters appears to be playing the same role as Group Research, Inc., the Democratic Party front that was used to help the Kennedy and Johnson Administrations target conservative radio broadcasters using the Fairness Doctrine in the 1960s. But Media Matters has scored a major success in the Imus case even without the Fairness Doctrine.

IMUS VS. HILLARY

Although Imus was not a conservative, he was a critic of Hillary Clinton. And that made him a target for Media Matters.

As the Media Matters/Olbermann attack on Tumulty suggests, the Imus affair is all about politics and protecting Hillary. Imus, who endorsed and opposed candidates for office, including the presidency, was considered very influential. That is why so many politicians went on his show. He was beginning to emerge as a major thorn in the side of Hillary, just as her competition with Senator Barack Obama for the Democratic presidential nomination was heating up.

While Imus had allowed Obama to come on his show, he had steadfastly refused to permit Senator Clinton to appear. Imus had been on the outs with the Clintons for many years, with some of the hostility stemming from his performance at the Radio/TV Correspondents Association Annual Dinner in 1996. Among other things, Imus had made fun of the former president's womanizing.

Before he was fired by NBC News and CBS, one of Imus's sidekicks regularly imitated Bill Clinton on the air, reminding people of how this potential First Husband had become a first class national embarrassment and disgrace when he was having sexual relations with a former White House intern and lied about it. It was one of the truly funny bits on the show.

If you think the Hillary connection to the Imus firing is a stretch, consider the fact that David Brock wrote a sympathetic book about Hillary during the time of his transition from closeted homosexual to ex-conservative.

A RELATIONSHIP WITH HILLARY'S PRESS AIDE

As Reed Irvine and I noted in an article back in 2002, "Brock got a million-dollar advance for a book on Hillary Clinton, but while writing it, he underwent a transformation. Instead of an exposé, the book was so soft on Hillary that it bombed. In two Esquire articles, Brock repudiated his Clinton muckraking and apologized to the president. His flip-flop appears to have been related to the close relationship that Brock, a closeted homosexual, established with Hillary's openly gay press secretary, Neel Lattimore." *The Advocate,* a homosexual magazine, had described Lattimore as one of Hillary's "closest confidants" during her White House years.

This is the same Neel Lattimore, according to the September 7, 2006, article by Glenn Thrush of *Newsday,* who would become "special projects director" for Media Matters.

Thrush also reported that "Kelly Craighead, one of the Clintons' closest friends, served as one of Brock's top advisers during Media Matters' formation in 2004. She was paid as part of a $202,781 contract with her husband, Erick Mullen's, consulting company, tax records obtained by Newsday show." Craighead had served as assistant to President Clinton and director of the advance team for then-First Lady Hillary Rodham Clinton. It is reported that when Craighead married political consultant Erick Mullen, a former aide to Senator Charles Schumer, in 2001, Hillary Clinton performed the civil ceremony. Mullen was an informal senior advisor to Mrs. Clinton's run for the Senate in 2000.

THE HILLARY NETWORK

More recently, Lattimore has emerged as an official spokesman for the Children's Defense Fund, headed by longtime Hillary friend Marian Wright Edelman. Hillary had served on the Board of Editors of Yale Law Review and Social Action and had interned with Edelman. After graduating from Yale, Hillary served as an adviser to the Children's Defense Fund and then as its chairperson from 1986 to 1992.

It is significant that, at the 2007 National Action Network Convention, hosted by Al Sharpton, the Friday "Women's Luncheon" featured Senator Clinton and Marian Wright Edelman.

For her part, Mrs. Clinton had denounced Imus's Rutgers comments as "bigotry and coarse sexism," adding, "I've never wanted to go on his show and I certainly don't ever intend to go on his show, and I felt that way before his latest outrageous, hateful, hurtful comments."

For his part, Obama denounced Imus and called for his firing. He had to do this, considering the pressure on Imus being exerted by Sharpton and Jesse Jackson. But Obama may have lost a valuable ally. Imus had supported John Kerry for president in 2004 and regularly denounced Bush Administration officials as "war criminals" for their conduct of the Iraq War. His views on Iraq were in tune with those of Obama and, despite his long-time backing for Republican Senator John McCain, Imus may have been laying the groundwork for supporting Obama, at least in the Democratic presidential primaries, in 2008.

WHO BENEFITS?

Perhaps that is the main reason why, after years of insulting scores of people, with the quiet acquiescence of so many in the liberal media, the latest insult was seized upon and proved to be his undoing. In terms of who benefits politically from Imus going off the air, Hillary Clinton emerges above all others, even above Sharpton and Jackson.

Media Matters, which openly supports the return of the so-called Fairness Doctrine in order to muzzle conservatives, will now move on to its next target. One thing is certain: it will be a political opponent of Senator Clinton.

Clinton, a presidential candidate, has taken no public stand on the return of the Fairness Doctrine. But she has been accused by a colleague, Senator James Inhofe, of supporting legislative action against talk radio.

On Thursday June 21, 2007, Senator James Inhofe (R-OK) appeared on the John Ziegler evening show on KFI 640 AM in Los Angeles. Inhofe discussed with Ziegler a conversation he overheard, and then joined, with Senators Clinton and Barbara Boxer where they discussed the need for a "legislative fix" to "have balance" in talk radio after complaining about talk radio being "nothing but far-right-wing extremists."

On June 22, 2007, Inhofe was on Sean Hannity's radio program, explaining that he misspoke, and that he overheard the Clinton and Boxer conversation three years ago, not "the other day," as he told Ziegler. But the date of the conversation was not as important as the conversation itself. Inhofe was saying that Clinton and Boxer wanted federal government interference in radio programming.

Inhofe retold the story, which he said he had told "at least a hundred times," about the conversation he overheard "on an elevator going up to vote." He said he overheard Senators Clinton and Boxer saying, "All we ever hear is extreme right-wing stuff on these radio shows. We got to do something about it, there's got to be a fix to this thing."

In response, Inhofe told Boxer and Clinton, "You girls don't understand, it's market driven, and there's no market for your liberal tripe." Inhofe then told Hannity, "Liberals don't understand that there aren't people out there who are just waiting for them to come up with a great liberal audience that can join in."

On Hannity's program, the conversation got more in-depth, with Hannity asking Inhofe about a report from the Center for American Progress, a George Soros-funded group, on diversity in radio programming.

Hannity noted that the group is led by "Hillary's front man John Podesta," who had served as Bill Clinton's chief of staff. Hannity said the report included "a lot of recommendations, all government regulations, to intimidate radio owners and station groups," adding, "there's other talk about bringing back the Fairness Doctrine."

CLINTON AND BOXER ISSUE DENIALS

Clinton and Boxer deny the conversation described by Inhofe ever took place, with Boxer saying, "Senator Inhofe either needs new glasses or needs to have his hearing checked because the conversation never happened."

Clinton spokesman Philippe Reines responded, "Jim Inhofe is wrong. This supposed conversation never happened, not in his presence or anywhere else."

Inhofe said he wasn't really surprised that the two would deny the conversation took place. But he said that he hears Democrats complaining about conservative talk radio all the time.

When asked by Hannity if he believed the Fairness Doctrine would return, Inhofe asked, "Do these people want to do the same thing with CNN? Do they want to do the same thing with the networks?" He then added, "I don't think there's a chance it would pass because you guys are going to do your job and make sure there is such a thing as the First Amendment."

However, as AIM has demonstrated, the chances of a Democratic president and Congress getting the Fairness Doctrine passed into law are actually very good.

But the Fairness Doctrine is not the only item on the liberal agenda. Another is opposition to what they call "media consolidation." Everybody is opposed to concentration of media properties in a few hands. But the Left uses the phrase "media consolidation" to describe how conservative-oriented broadcasters are getting more powerful and influential. The Left wants limits on the number of radio stations and media properties that conservatives can own or control.

For his part, Hannity acknowledged that liberals will continue to push for the Fairness Doctrine and for more government regulation to force more liberal voices on the air. He talked of a "blueprint... to structurally shift through regulation ownership rules to silence talk radio, or to force stations to take programs that they don't want..." Hannity added, "There's a direct assault on the First Amendment from a lot of corners going on now."

HILLARY'S ALLIES

Also on Fox News, Alan Colmes wondered why, if what Inhofe alleged was true, Clinton and Boxer had not acted against talk radio. "What have Hillary Clinton and Barbara Boxer done in the last three years to advance this legislatively?" Colmes asked.

In fact, as AIM has documented, Clinton has relied on a front organization, Media Matters, to help advance her agenda in the media. Media Matters head David Brock has called for the return of the Fairness Doctrine. In fact, Brock's Media Matters was reported to be behind a website, fairnessdoctrine.com, which was specifically set up in support of a bill by Rep. Louise Slaughter (D-NY) to reinstate the Fairness Doctrine. The website has since been taken down.

Writing about fairnessdoctrine.com, James Gattuso noted that the site was "co-sponsored by Andrew Jay Schwartzman of the Democracy Access Project, David Brock of Media Matters, and Tom Athans of Democracy Radio."

Athans, co-founder and former CEO of Democracy Radio, is an interesting figure who may stand to benefit if the federal government mandates the sale or breakup of media properties. Athans, who also served as an official of the liberal Air America radio network, is the husband of Michigan Democratic Senator Debbie Stabenow. He developed and produced the liberal Ed Schultz and Stephanie Miller radio shows.

LIBERAL MCCAIN BOOSTER

AIM discovered that fairnessdoctrine.com was registered to Nicco Mele, the webmaster for Howard Dean's 2004 presidential campaign and co-founder of EchoDitto, an organization that creates "vibrant online communities." Its projects include the Rosie O'Donnell blog and the Clinton Global Initiative website.

Ironically, Mele made statements in support of John McCain's presidential run. "A lot of people are asking me about John McCain," Mele wrote. "When I worked for Common Cause, I worked on the McCain-Feingold bill and worked closely with Sen. John McCain's office. After Sen. McCain lost the Republican primary in 2000, I traveled with him as part of a group of campaign finance reform staffers as we criss-crossed the country working to secure support for the McCain-Feingold bill. I have long admired Sen. McCain's work on campaign finance reform and his independent streak. If Sen. McCain runs for president, he's got my support."

AIR AMERICA SEES GREEN

Meanwhile, the liberal Air America radio network has been re-launched, after going through bankruptcy, with support from such figures as Bill and Hillary Clinton. The network was sold in March, 2007, to Green Family Media, run by the Green family. Stephen Green became chairman of the board and Mark Green became president of the new Air America.

Bill Clinton appeared in the Air America "relaunch video" and Hillary was interviewed on the air when the new owners took charge. "You are really important," Bill Clinton told them. "This is a big deal."

Mark Green was on Fox News Sunday on July 1, declaring that progressives were really not interested in bringing back the Fairness Doctrine. He said, "I don't want the government to mandate speech." But he also said that a station should go through a "license renewal proceeding" and represent "diverse communities."

Green's comments were denounced as doubletalk by some conservatives. But his remarks were consistent with what we know about Democratic plans to bring back the Fairness Doctrine. They know they can't get it back under the Bush Administration so they've figured that it's better not to talk about it. That is why so many joined in the 309-115 vote in favor of the Pence amendment.

THE PLAN

It's better, from the liberal point of view, to use this time to talk about community involvement, diversity, and the licensing procedures for broadcasters which already exist. It also makes sense to hold hearings or conduct studies on the matter, such as what Rep. John Dingell is doing. Dingell, chairman of the House Commerce Committee, which has jurisdiction over the Pence Broadcaster Freedom Act, has requested a federal study of how broadcasters encourage "hate crimes."

This process could lay the groundwork for bringing back the Fairness Doctrine or even mandating the sale of various broadcasting properties to people like the Greens and Tom Athans. But that will only happen when a Democratic president is in the White House and the FCC is safely in Democratic hands.

Liberals are biding their time, thinking that time is on their side.

VII

FAIR & BALANCED?
WHO DECIDES?

BY LYNN WOOLLEY

"Oh, God I wish I hadn't said that!"

As a talk show host, I am among an exclusive group that actually CAN take back an intemperate comment made in the heat of the moment. I have exactly ten seconds to make that decision.

For fifteen hours each week, I sit in front of a broadcast console —VU meters to the front, a telephone to the left, and my right finger never far from what is affectionately known as the "dump button."

Truth be told it's usually a caller that gets dumped as in this actual example: "Lynn, I just can't deal with those f...ing liberals anymore." That's a dump for sure. But there has been a time that I've actually dumped something I've said. And time and again, I deal with the split-second decision making process over how far I should let a listener or guest go.

But it's MY decision to make.

For the past twelve years, it's been up to me to push that button that erases the past ten seconds—usually to defuse an errant F-bomb —or simply to say to a caller: "Look, Tom, I see where you're taking this and I just don't want to go there." Sometimes, it's a matter of having been a reporter in a prior life and saying to Fred in Austin: "You're making some accusations without any evidence. We don't deal in rumors on this show."

Back in Dallas, when I was a young news lion, we called it "broadcast judgment." That is, a seasoned reporter or anchor instinctively knew when something crossed the line of fairness and responsibility.

I'm only 57 years old at this writing—and a young 57 at that—but my news background in big radio markets like Dallas and Austin, coupled with the fact that I'm one of the few talk show hosts that's worked in the medium both pre-and-post Fairness Doctrine, gives me a unique perspective on the issue of regulation.

WHEN TALK RADIO WAS BORING

I remember the days when political talk on-air was little more than public affairs, broadcast simply to fulfill FCC service commitments. I remember when talk show hosts acted as "traffic cops" directing calls, but advancing no opinions of their own. And I revel in the current days of free, unlimited speech that we all enjoy on the radio today. I want to keep it that way.

During the Reagan years, on a 100,000-watt FM rocker in Waco, my on-air partner, Steve Cannon, and I created voice-characters so that we could get away with political commentary. We knew that if we came on the air with explicit political commentary, we'd be in trouble with the management, the government or both. So our characters—not us personally—took jabs at the politicians we wished to comment on. Or, in the case of President Reagan whom we supported, the characters would slip in comedic comments that left little doubt regarding our support of Reagan's policies. Remember that political parody is protected, which is how Paul Shanklin gets away with his politically charged remakes of popular songs.

Had Lynn Woolley and Steve Cannon made the statements in our own voices that our characters made, we could have been subject to regulation. Understand that we were doing a radio team show on a Top 40 station—not a political talk show. But even so, we were careful to couch our comments in the arena of comedy. Did the station get complaints? Oh, yes. One sponsor threatened to pull out and several prominent officials complained from time to time.

Before the end of Reagan's term, the Fairness Doctrine was gone and radio was truly a free medium.

Hooked on Rush

One day, while driving, I heard Rush Limbaugh for the first time. He was in the middle of what we in radio call a "bit"—this one was a monologue on abortion.

"I have a phone call," said Rush [paraphrasing from memory here!] "...and I'm not sure what to do with it. I would like to take this call, but the timing is not convenient. I am tempted to do away with this call, to not take it at all. I have other things on my agenda and this call came totally unexpected."

I had never heard Rush before, but I immediately caught on to what he was doing.

"While it would inconvenience me to take this call, I can't help but wonder what would happen if I do take it. Who knows? The call may have potential. The call might actually amount to something. If I don't take this call, I'll never know what it might have been."

That was great radio, a perfect analogy—and I was hooked. A few years later, when the chance arose, I jumped into the talk medium. Many years and hundreds of hours later, I'm still doing it. Am I as good as Rush? You're damn right I am. [Wait! DUMP BUTTON!]

Ladies and gentlemen, I'm glad you didn't have to hear that. Fact is, Rush started this New Media and I'm just a follower. That I have the ability to express my views and take telephone calls, and feature guests—all of whom can speak their minds without fear of government intervention—is Rush's legacy and a part of what makes the United States of America a great country.

Progressive Talk—Low Ratings

Unfortunately, the fact that Rush Limbaugh has been so successful is also the reason that the medium he largely created is in constant danger. It would actually be advantageous, in a way, to on-air conservatives if a liberal Limbaugh were to emerge. Ed Schultz has perhaps come the closest, but his audience is negligible in comparison to Limbaugh's just as the total audience for "progressive" talk is virtually non-existent when compared to the conservative audience. Air America, and even big broadcast corporations like Clear Channel have tried. If a few progressive hosts caught on and pulled enough ratings numbers to succeed, then maybe the clamor on the Left for the Fairness Doctrine's return would subside.

That would be the free marketplace at work. Ah, but the market is working NOW; it's just that the market doesn't seem to want liberal talk. So under President Democrat, it is quite likely that the government will seek to go around the marketplace.

LEFT, RIGHT, LEFT, RIGHT, LEFT, RIGHT...

Imagine this exchange on a major national talk show:

HOST: Our topic today is the War in Iraq. John in Walla Walla, what's your take on this?

CALLER: Well, Michael [a vast number of talk hosts seem to be named 'Michael'] I believe we ought to fight to win. We can't let al Qaeda get a foothold there.

HOST: All right, John, thanks for the call. John says we stay. How about you? Let's go to Sarah in Pensacola.

CALLER: Michael, that last caller is so wrong. Our troops are nothing more than sitting ducks over there. Bush got us into this, and we need to get out.

HOST: Sarah wants us to get out. Let's see what Jim in Oklahoma City thinks. Jim, you're on the Michael Michaels Show.

CALLER: Hi, Michael. Well, I think we have to stay. Otherwise, the United States' reputation around the world will be diminished forever.

HOST: And how about Virginia in Sacramento?

CALLER: This is Virginia. Michael, our reputation around the world is already diminished.

This is a fictional exchange, but not too far off from what political talk radio used to be prior to the Fairness Doctrine—IF you could find a political talk show anywhere on the dial. This is an example of the talk show host as "traffic cop"—directing calls but rarely if ever putting forth an opinion of his or her own. It's simply a matter of "what do you think" followed by the next call and the same question—"what do you think"!

You'll also note that the screener, under the Fairness Doctrine, may very well feel the need to "balance" the calls with a "pro" and a "con" assuming that there are still callers once talk radio becomes this boring.

Broadcasters might find other ways to be "fair and balanced."

Perhaps Rush Limbaugh could be left intact in his midday slot. And then let's say that the radio station followed Rush with three hours of a progressive such as Jim Hightower or Mario Cuomo. Would the Left accept that?

The answer is no.

Remember that on cable television, where Fox New Channel is perceived as conservative, CNN as neutral, and MSNBC as liberal—the Left is still outraged because FNC has more viewers. They want to regulate O'Reilly and Hannity because fewer people are watching Matthews and Olbermann.

By that standard, if the same radio station carried Limbaugh and got the usual high ratings numbers—and then followed with a liberal, be it Schultz, Bill Press or anyone else—the liberal would need to have the exact same listening level as Rush or it would not be "balanced."

WE HAVE WAYS TO MAKE YOU LISTEN

Liberals not only want to dish it out. They want YOU to listen to it. If you don't, then something must be wrong by their reasoning, and government must step in.

You may be thinking—so what? If the radio station balances Rush Limbaugh with three hours of a liberal in a comparable time-slot, and that satisfies the Doctrine under the current interpretation, then the Left would have to leave it alone.

If that's what you think, then you don't know the Left. When the Left gets mad, the Left goes to court.

Remember that if Plan A doesn't work, liberals will resort to Plan B. And Plan B may be even more devious.

ALLRED IS ALL WRONG

Here's an example, contained in a letter from the ultra-leftist Los Angeles lawyer and talk show host Gloria Allred that was carried in the September 27, 2000 edition of the Dallas Morning News. Gloria was upset with Dr. Laura Schlessinger with regard to comments about the gay and lesbian lifestyle and was looking for a way to shut her up. Since Gloria had no Fairness Doctrine to work with, and since Dr. Laura obviously enjoyed freedom of speech, Gloria resorted to accusations of discrimination:

"Gays and lesbians also have a right to be free of discrimination and to exercise their free speech in response to hers. Dr. Laura's statements are produced in a California workplace: a television studio. California law prohibits discrimination based on sexual orientation in the workplace. If she makes discriminatory statements on her show she may end up with a lawsuit that would teach her an expensive lesson. Employees have the right to be free of discrimination so they can enjoy equal employment opportunity. Statements of prejudice interfere with that right."

This is a chilling statement.

It's not so much that Gloria is any danger to anyone; it's the mere idea that liberals and the PC crowd will search until they find a way to silence any language they disagree with. It's like that episode of the Twilight Zone where the omnipotent kid would turn you into a scarecrow for thinking bad thoughts. Gloria Allred would turn Dr. Laura into a former talk show host for daring to disagree with—Gloria Allred.

(It should be pointed out here that Dr. Laura's position is amazingly mainstream. She states that homosexuality is not normal and that it is often a destructive lifestyle. Until the PC movement declared otherwise, this was the prevailing thought in most religions and in most civilized areas of the world. You don't have to hate homosexuals to be disgusted by what the term implies. Besides, Dr. Laura is taking a stand against a certain behavior that she disagrees with. If we now have "behavior rights," then wait for the pedophiles to start coming out of the woodwork. Why not? No one will be able to speak out against them lest he or she be accused of "behavior discrimination.")

In short, a broadcast world in which the Fairness Doctrine has been reinstated will be tedious with many forms for stations and hosts to fill out. Proving that a station or an individual show is "fair and balanced" will be the order of the day. The on-air product will be sterile compared to what we're used to. Courthouses will be filled with cases asking judges and juries to decide whose interpretation of the rules is correct. The Left will pour on the lawsuits in the hope that radio companies will tire of the expense of litigation, and simply stop airing opinion shows.

Some of them will.

VIII

FINDING A LIBERAL RUSH LIMBAUGH

BY LYNN WOOLLEY

One reason that "progressives" are so eager to return to the Fairness Doctrine is their abject failure to find and groom a talk show host of the Left that can be as compelling as Rush Limbaugh. It's not for lack of trying.

There have been many attempts to bring a non-radio celebrity—usually a retired Democratic politician or a Hollywood comedian—and train that person to become the "liberal Rush Limbaugh." There have also been attempts to build entire networks around progressive hosts. Most of these attempts have not worked out and the fact remains that, to this day, there is no liberal Rush Limbaugh.

An early announcement of what would become "Air America" was carried by the Associated Press on February 17, 2003. The headline read, "Capitalists plan liberal network."

Jon Sinton was tabbed to be the chief executive of the fledgling network, and he was giddy about the prospects for success: "We believe this is a tremendous business opportunity," he was quoted as saying in the release. "There are so many right-wing talk shows, we think it's created a hole in the market you could drive a truck through."

The group of investors was led by multi-millionaire venture capitalist Sheldon Drobney and his wife Anita. The company was initially known as AnShell Media, L.L.C., and was claiming it had $10 million upfront, while seeking more from other wealthy supporters of the Democratic Party or progressive causes.

Sinton mentioned Bill and Hillary Clinton by name, saying that "those who lean to the right are great at haranguing [the Clintons] but those who lean left have better connections to the entertainment world in Hollywood and New York."

So this explains the attraction of Air America to comedians such as Al Franken and Janeane Garofalo. It also helps to explain why liberal networks fail. So-called comedians such as Franken live for cheap laughs. During an on-stage monologue, most comedians would want to keep the audience in stitches with a funny line every ten seconds. But radio is different.

First, there must be a serious side. In the case of Rush Limbaugh, the audience is treated to various one-liners and parodies, but it's Rush's monologues that make his show so highly rated. Rush knows how to strike the perfect balance between the serious and the absurd, mostly because he is a lifelong radio professional who understands the medium.

Second, most comedians work on a circuit and play to different audiences on different days. But on radio, much of the same audience is back every day. Different people tune in and out, but the audience is static enough that a host simply cannot use the same comedy lines over and over.

Third, and perhaps most important, talk radio is long-form entertainment. Most radio talk shows are three hours long. This presents special problems for people like Franken who aren't used to performing fifteen solid hours per week. It takes a lot of material, very little of which can be used more than once. And, people like Franken despise being chained to a microphone constantly because it limits their ability to go on the road with their respective shows.

By depending on Hollywood types for talent, the new liberal network was starting out in a hole.

A BRIEF HISTORY OF AIR AMERICA

It was most likely late 2002 when the Drobneys decided to move forward with the idea of a progressive radio network, perhaps after being encouraged by Bill Clinton and Al Gore. In fact, Drobney even says it was Gore who introduced him to Franken.

After the announcement of AnShell Media, the Drobneys sold the company to Evan Cohen and Mark Walsh and it was renamed "Progress Media." In January of 2004, Progress Media signed Franken and Robert F. Kennedy, Jr., and later signed Janeane Garofalo and Randi Rhodes.

"Central Air," as it had been called, was renamed "Air America" and signed on March 31, 2004. It had affiliates in New York, Los Angeles, San Bernardino and Portland, Oregon. A few other stations were listed as affiliates, but it soon came out that Air America was leasing time of some of these stations, as opposed to Rush Limbaugh's management company which charges stations for airing Rush.

No sooner had Air America begun broadcasting than it was embroiled in controversies—part of which may have been due to lack of sufficient capital.

Just two weeks in, a radio company called "Multicultural Radio" pulled Air America's programming in two big markets—Chicago and Santa Monica in the Los Angeles metro area. The network charged that Multicultural had sold time on the LA station to another party, and that was why Air America stopped payment on checks. But Multicultural claimed that an Air America check had bounced and said that the network owed more than $1 million. Air America went to court, ultimately losing and being ordered to pay $250,000 in damages and attorneys' fees.

Air America was also plagued by defections. Just four weeks in, CEO Mark Walsh and a programming executive named Dave Logan left. A week after that, Evan Cohen and his investment partner Rex Sorensen left as well.

The network went through a reorganization during which investors in Progress Media bought the assets of the company and created Piquant, L.L.C. In February, 2005, Danny Goldberg signed on as the new CEO and in April, 2005, Gary Krantz became president. By the middle of 2006, both Goldberg and Krantz had left. There were also big changes in the on-air lineup. Janeane Garofalo was out as of July 14, 2006. On August 30, 2006, the network fired its evening host, Mike Malloy. And Franken himself left as of February 14, 2007 to run for the Senate in Minnesota. Other controversies emerged including one involving the Gloria Wise Boys and Girls Club, a non-profit outfit that provides services to children and the elderly in the Bronx. A posting on wizbangblog.com on July 28, 2005 was entitled "Air America's charity scam denials don't ring true," and took the network to task for receiving almost half a million dollars in loans from the organization that "Air America owners don't seem to remember anymore." The blog accused the network of deliberately reorganizing the company in order to avoid having to repay the loans and other liabilities. Wikipedia states that Evan Cohen was also the Director of Development for Gloria Wise, and says that while this case remains under investigation, Air America has now repaid the loan.

Air America's much-publicized Chapter 11 bankruptcy filing took place on October 13, 2006. Court records showed the network with assets of about $4.3 million and liabilities of $20.2 million—part of which was a whopping $360,750 still owed to Al Franken. There were more than twenty-five pages of creditors. The network had lost $9.1 million in 2004; $19.6 million in 2005; and $13.1 million by October 2006.

January 29, 2007 brought a letter of intent from a prospective new owner: SLG Radio L.L.C., with Stephen L. Green at the helm. Green created "Green Family Media" and once the sale went through on March 6, 2007, he named his brother Mark J. Green to be the network's chairman.

The Greens brought in veteran WOR/New York programmer David Bernstein to be in charge of Air America's on-air content. Bernstein told the New York Daily News, "I don't see our purpose as 'answering' conservative radio or Rush Limbaugh. There's no clear majority in this country today. We want to talk to everyone and help everyone make the right choice."

And so Air America rolls on, doing all right in some liberal towns like Portland, but with just a fraction of the audience of conservative talk radio.

THE SEARCH GOES ON

On June 21, 2007, a major joint report was issued by two organizations—the Center for American Progress and the Free Press—entitled "The Structural Imbalance of Political Talk Radio." The purpose of the report was not only to use a statistical analysis to confirm what every radio listener already knows—that conservatives dominate talk radio—but also to show how that domination could be ended.

The report purported to show the following:

- Of 257 news/talk radio stations owned by the top five owners, 91 percent of the total weekday talk programming was conservative as of Spring 2007.
- Each weekday, 2,570 hours and fifteen minutes of conservative talk are broadcast compared to 254 hours of liberal talk—a factor of ten to one.
- 76 percent of news/talk programming in the top ten U.S. radio markets is conservative while 24 percent is liberal.

Interestingly enough, the report did not single out the Fairness Doctrine as the major reason for this terrible "imbalance." Neither did it place the blame on market forces—you know, that nasty idea that people have the freedom to tune in to whatever program they desire.

Rather, the study concluded that the gap between conservative and liberal radio was due to "structural programs in the U.S. regulatory system" and the breakdown of the public trustee concept of broadcasting. The report decried the "elimination of clear public interest requirements for broadcasting, and the relaxation of ownership rules including the requirement of local participation in management..."

Now with regard to the issue of ownership consolidation, you will find mixed reaction within the industry that has virtually no relation to political leanings. Those who have profited from media consolidation (generally the large companies like Clear Channel and top-line hosts whose shows are owned by those companies) will sing its praises, while those who have lost their jobs to it will curse it.

But few in the business want to return to the days in which certain programming is mandated in the name of "the public interest" that no one will listen to.

Even so, it is interesting to find one's name—in this case Lynn Woolley—among the list of conservative hosts "examined," or perhaps more correctly put, "targeted" by the study.

Several pages of the study are devoted to methodology—and you'd have to be a statistician or a mathematician to understand it. The bottom line, though, is easy to comprehend: We need less conservative talk radio and more liberals on the air.

Oh, so?

One of the names listed on this study is one Paul "Woody" Woodhull—a name familiar to those who know the background of liberal talk radio. And our man Woody is hardly an unbiased statistician.

Google the name and you'll find that he's a radio talk show veteran and president of Media Syndication Services, Inc., located in Washington, D.C. A bio at talkprogress.com claims that Woody has been behind several successful programs. One of those shows happens to be the closest thing yet the liberals have come to finding their leftist Limbaugh.

We're talking about the Ed Schultz Show, heard on about 90 stations (as opposed to Rush's more than 600) through "Big Eddie Radio Productions, L.L.C." Woodhull is listed as one of the founders of "Big Eddie" and responsible for signing the talent, designing the business plan, and negotiating with a syndicator. Woodhull negotiated the sale of "Big Eddie" to "Product First," a company owned by Randy Michaels, the former CEO of Clear Channel. Woodhull is also a founding member of "Bill Press Partners" that produces "The Bill Press Show." You'll remember Press as the liberal half of CNN's "Crossfire" for a time.

Woodhull was tapped as a judge in yet another "search for the liberal Limbaugh"—this time a contest put on by Clear Channel, the Center for American Progress Action Fund (remember them from the study?), and Jones Radio Network, the company that syndicates Schultz. On September 9, 2006, the group used Schultz's website to announce "a nationwide search for the next progressive talk radio star." "Progressive talk has grown so big, so fast, that all of us in the industry are searching high and low for more great progressive talk radio talent," said Woody. "Great talkers like Ed Schultz and Bill Press, and Al Franken are hard to find."

Indeed. And perhaps that's why Mr. Woodhull lent his name and expertise to a study whose goal was to utilize regulation rather than "great progressive talent" to even up the political landscape on your radio dial.

REGULATION, THE VENEZUELAN WAY

Just how far apart today's "progressives" are from outright socialists like Venezuela's emerging dictator Hugo Chavez, is a matter of opinion. But, like American liberals, Chavez would much rather tune into TV and radio and hear his own government-approved point-of-view.

In May 2007, the wires were full of stories about Chavez closing down an openly anti-government TV channel known as Radio Caracas Television (RCTV). The privately owned network carried popular comedy and drama shows, but wasn't shy in its criticism of the government. Chavez also accused Venezuelan TV network Globovision of encouraging any would-be assassins of the president. RCTV was replaced on the air by TVes, a state-backed "socialist" station that began showing cultural programming. A dispatch carried on Yahoo News said that Chavez supporters held a "huge, night-to-dawn public party" celebrating the birth of the new "socialist television" and the end of the "bitterly anti-Chavez" media outlet.

The Yahoo report said that the RCTV closure was not well received either inside or outside the country. A leading Venezuelan newspaper, El Nacional, called it "the end of pluralism in Venezuela," and said the government was establishing an "information monopoly." An archbishop in Merida compared Chavez to Hitler, Mussolini, and even his friend Fidel Castro.

Sounding like Clinton in the wake of Oklahoma City, Chavez was reported by the Associated Press as saying that radio stations should not be inciting violence by "manipulating feelings" among the populace. Chavez even threatened to file charges against CNN for linking him to Al Qaeda.

All of this led to protests, particularly over the closure of RCTV. On the Monday following the shutdown, several people were injured as Caracas police fired rubber bullets and tear gas to quash a demonstration in support of the closed network.

Could something such as this happen in the United States? Would the American people take to the streets and protest if liberals were able to remove Rush Limbaugh or Sean Hannity from the air as they did with Don Imus? Remember that the study from the Center for American Progress seeks to use government to effectively dismantle the political radio landscape as we know it. That's not exactly what's happening in Venezuela, but it's too close for comfort.

What is happening right now in our very own hemisphere is the ultimate result of a regulatory or Fairness Doctrine mentality.

APPENDIX: LEGISLATIVE ACTION AND ROLL CALL ON VOTE TO STOP THE FAIRNESS DOCTRINE

On June 28, 2007, the Rep. Mike Pence amendment was adopted by a vote of 309-115 and added to the Financial Services Appropriations bill. It prohibits funds from being used by the Federal Communications Commission to impose the Fairness Doctrine on broadcasters. But it only applies to fiscal year 2008 dollars and there is no plan by the current Republican-dominated FCC to reimpose the doctrine.

Pence himself pointed out that "Although my amendment to the Financial Services Appropriations bill passed, prohibiting any funding to the FCC for the enforcement of the Fairness Doctrine, should it be resurrected, we must keep in mind that it is only a one-year moratorium on funding. While I am pleased that 309 Members of Congress supported this short-term fix, it is my hope that they will continue to stand for freedom of speech by joining me in a long-term solution to the problem by passing the Broadcaster Freedom Act."

On the House floor, after Pence introduced and explained his amendment, Democratic Rep. Jose Serrano declared that "...I would just like to inform the gentleman that we will accept his amendment." Serrano voted for it.

In other words, Democrats were prepared to let it pass without debate or opposition.

But a debate ensued anyway.

The debate may have served a purpose if it raised awareness by the public about what Democrats have planned—and that more action to protect the First Amendment is urgently needed.

Democratic Rep. David Obey pointed out that "...the totally Republican-dominated commission is not going to resurrect that doctrine." Even Obey voted for the Pence amendment.

Rep. Diane Watson said that the Pence amendment was designed to "prevent spending on something that doesn't exist." Watson voted against it.

Rep. Dennis Kucinich said the debate over the Pence amendment was "a red herring" because the Bush Administration "would never reinstate" the Fairness Doctrine anyway. He said, "It's a debate about something that's not going to happen under this administration, but it may happen under a future administration." Kucinich voted against the Pence amendment.

Rep. John D. Dingell called the Pence amendment "entirely unnecessary," noting that "I understand from the Federal Communications Commission (FCC) chairman's office that the FCC has no plans to even debate the issue, much less take action. In other words, there will be no action at the FCC on the Fairness Doctrine. It is therefore unclear why the gentleman—who must know this fact—is even offering the amendment." Dingell voted against it.

The critical matter, which Pence acknowledges, is a long-term solution. Unfortunately, the chances of a Democratic-controlled House and Senate passing Pence's Broadcaster Freedom Act are considered to be slim or none because it would tie the hands of a possible Democratic president who could appoint a Democratic FCC majority. And that majority could reinstate the Fairness Doctrine.

Can a liberal-controlled Congress be forced to safeguard First Amendment rights by passing the Broadcaster Freedom Act? That is the tremendous challenge ahead. Conservatives should not be misled by erroneous media coverage into thinking that passage of the Pence amendment by an overwhelming margin solved the problem. It did not. It is symbolic and largely irrelevant.

When a Democratic president appoints the chairman of the FCC, the Democrats will have a 3-2 majority. Hillary Clinton's backers in the Media Matters group want the return of the Fairness Doctrine so they can enlist FCC bureaucrats in the effort to control and influence the content of conservative talk radio.

House Debate, June 28, 2007.

(From the Congressional Record, roll call vote at end of debate.)

Mr. PENCE. Mr. Chairman, I come to the floor today, along with my partners in this amendment, Congressman JEB HENSARLING of Texas, Congressman JEFF FLAKE of Arizona, very much in a spirit of bipartisanship. We come to the floor in this moment, on this amendment, to be about that which I think we are all about.

The freedom of speech and the freedom of the press is not a partisan issue in this Congress. We all live under and cherish that First Amendment that says Congress shall make no law abridging the freedom of speech or of the press.

I, myself, Mr. Chairman, have worked in a bipartisan way in this Congress to fashion legislation that ensures a free and independent press. The amendment before this body today is simply an extension of that mission.

Our legislation would simply say that none of the funds made available in this act may be used by the Federal Communications Commission to implement the Fairness Doctrine, as repealed in 1985.

Now, the Fairness Doctrine actually came to pass in 1949, part of a regulation of a much older law. It required broadcasters to present controversial issues in a fair and balanced manner. That sounds reasonable enough. But because of the lack of clarity in the regulation, in the commission's rulings, broadcasters, during almost four decades, often opted not to offer any controversial programming whatsoever.

The FCC concluded that in fact, by 1985, this regulation was having a chilling effect on the public debate and repealed it effective 1987. Since the demise of the Fairness Doctrine, talk radio particularly has emerged as a dynamic forum for public debate and, I offer, an asset to the Nation.

Our amendment, simply put, is an effort to maintain the status quo, to prevent this administration and this Federal Communications Commission, in this fiscal year about which we are debating, to use no funds to return the Fairness Doctrine.

Now, I want to acknowledge the fact that there are some who are skeptical about the need for this amendment. I have heard distinguished and respected Members of this body come to this floor and say that this is, quote, "an issue which does not exist," and have seen writing, and I expect we will hear rhetoric to that effect, and I will respect the words of each person that utters that view, but I will differ.

Just for example, in the last 2 days, the Senate majority whip, the distinguished Senator from Illinois, RICHARD DURBIN, said, "It's time to reinstitute the Fairness Doctrine." That was yesterday. In the last several days, the chairman of the Senate Rules Committee, Senator DIANNE FEINSTEIN, said she was looking at reviving the Fairness Doctrine. The Democrat nominee for the President of the United States in 2004, the distinguished Senator JOHN KERRY, said, "I think the Fairness Doctrine ought to be there," and he went on to say, "I also think the equal time doctrine ought to come back." Most recently, the Center for American Progress, a liberal think tank, published an entire report on what it called the "structural imbalance of political talk radio."

So you will forgive me if many of us sense there is afoot in the Nation's Capital a bit of a cool breeze on the freedom of the press and the freedom of expression on the airwaves. So we seize this opportunity in the appropriations process, with my partners, JEFF FLAKE and JEB HENSARLING, and hopefully a bipartisan majority in this Congress, to say yes to freedom and to reject, in this fiscal year, the power that we have in the spending bill, any funds to be spent to bring back this unfairness doctrine to American broadcasting law.

[ROLL NO. 599]
AYES—309

Aderholt
Akin
Alexander
Altmire
Andrews
Baca
Bachmann
Bachus
Baker
Barrett (SC)
Barrow
Bartlett (MD)
Barton (TX)
Bean
Berman
Biggert
Bilbray
Bilirakis
Bishop (NY)
Bishop (UT)
Blackburn
Blunt
Boehner
Bonner
Bono
Boozman
Bordallo
Boren
Boucher
Boustany
Boyd (FL)
Brady (TX)
Brown (SC)
Brown, Corrine
Brown-Waite, Ginny
Buchanan
Burgess
Burton (IN)

Buyer
Calvert
Camp (MI)
Campbell (CA)
Cannon
Cantor
Capito
Cardoza
Carnahan
Carson
Carter
Castle
Castor
Chabot
Chandler
Christensen
Coble
Cole (OK)
Conaway
Cooper
Costa
Costello
Courtney
Cramer
Crenshaw
Crowley
Cubin
Cuellar
Culberson
Cummings
Davis (AL)
Davis (KY)
Davis, David
Davis, Lincoln
Davis, Tom
Deal (GA)
DeGette
Delahunt
Dent
Diaz-Balart, L.

Diaz-Balart, M.
Dicks
Donnelly
Doolittle
Drake
Dreier
Duncan
Edwards
Ehlers
Ellsworth
Emanuel
Emerson
Engel
English (PA)
Etheridge
Everett
Faleomavaega
Fallin
Feeney
Ferguson
Flake
Fortenberry
Fossella
Foxx
Franks (AZ)
Frelinghuysen
Gallegly
Garrett (NJ)
Gerlach
Giffords
Gilchrest
Gillibrand
Gillmor
Gingrey
Gohmert
Goode
Goodlatte
Gordon
Granger
Graves

Green, Gene
Hall (TX)
Hare
Hastings (FL)
Hastings (WA)
Hayes
Heller
Hensarling
Herger
Herseth Sandlin
Hill
Hobson
Hoekstra
Holden
Hooley
Hulshof
Hunter
Inglis (SC)
Inslee
Israel
Issa
Jackson-Lee (TX)
Jindal
Johnson (IL)
Johnson, Sam
Jones (NC)
Jordan
Kagen
Keller
Kildee
Kind
King (IA)
King (NY)
Kingston
Kirk
Kline (MN)
Knollenberg
Kuhl (NY)
Lamborn
Lampson

Lantos
Latham
LaTourette
Lewis (CA)
Lewis (KY)
Linder
Lipinski
LoBiondo
Lucas
Lungren, Daniel E.
Lynch
Mack
Mahoney (FL)
Manzullo
Marchant
Marshall
Matheson
McCarthy (CA)
McCarthy (NY)
McCaul (TX)
McCotter
McCrery
McHenry
McHugh
McIntyre
McKeon
McMorris Rodgers
Meek (FL)
Meeks (NY)
Melancon
Mica
Michaud
Miller (FL)
Miller (MI)
Miller (NC)
Miller, Gary
Mitchell
Mollohan
Moore (KS)
Moran (KS)

Murphy (CT)
Murphy, Patrick
Murphy, Tim
Musgrave
Myrick
Napolitano
Neugebauer
Norton
Nunes
Oberstar
Obey
Paul
Pearce
Pence
Perlmutter
Peterson (MN)
Peterson (PA)
Petri
Pickering
Pitts
Platts
Poe
Pomeroy
Porter
Price (GA)
Pryce (OH)
Putnam
Radanovich
Rahall
Ramstad
Regula
Rehberg
Reichert
Renzi
Reyes
Reynolds
Rodriguez
Rogers (AL)
Rogers (KY)
Rogers (MI)

Rohrabacher
Ros-Lehtinen
Roskam
Ross
Rothman
Roybal-Allard
Royce
Ruppersberger
Rush
Ryan (OH)
Ryan (WI)
Salazar
Sali
Sarbanes
Saxton
Schmidt
Schwartz
Scott (GA)
Sensenbrenner
Serrano
Shadegg
Shays
Shea-Porter
Sherman
Shimkus
Shuler
Shuster
Simpson
Sires
Skelton
Smith (NE)
Smith (NJ)
Smith (TX)
Smith (WA)
Snyder
Souder
Space
Spratt
Stearns
Stupak

Sullivan
Tancredo
Tanner
Taylor
Terry
Thornberry
Tiahrt
Tiberi
Turner
Udall (CO)
Udall (NM)
Upton
Visclosky
Walberg
Walden (OR)
Walsh (NY)
Walz (MN)
Wamp
Weiner
Weldon (FL)
Weller
Westmoreland
Whitfield
Wicker
Wilson (NM)
Wilson (OH)
Wilson (SC)
Wolf
Yarmuth
Young (AK)
Young (FL)

NOES—115
Ackerman
Allen
Arcuri
Baird
Baldwin
Becerra
Berkley

Berry
Bishop (GA)
Blumenauer
Boswell
Boyda (KS)
Brady (PA)
Braley (IA)
Butterfield
Capps
Capuano
Carney
Clarke
Clay
Cleaver
Clyburn
Conyers
Davis (CA)
Davis (IL)
DeFazio
DeLauro
Dingell
Doggett
Doyle
Ellison
Eshoo
Farr
Fattah
Filner
Frank (MA)
Gonzalez
Green, Al
Grijalva
Gutierrez
Hall (NY)
Harman
Higgins
Hinchey
Hirono
Hodes
Holt

Honda
Hoyer
Jackson (IL)
Jefferson
Johnson (GA)
Johnson, E. B.
Jones (OH)
Kanjorski
Kaptur
Kennedy
Kilpatrick
Klein (FL)
Kucinich
Langevin
Larsen (WA)
Larson (CT)
Lee
Levin
Lewis (GA)
Loebsack
Lofgren, Zoe
Lowey
Maloney (NY)
Markey
Matsui
McCollum (MN)
McDermott
McGovern
McNerney
Meehan
Miller, George
Moore (WI)
Moran (VA)
Murtha

Nadler
Neal (MA)
Olver
Pallone
Pascrell
Pastor
Payne
Price (NC)
Rangel
Sánchez, Linda T.
Sanchez, Loretta
Schakowsky
Schiff
Scott (VA)
Sestak
Slaughter
Solis
Stark
Sutton
Tauscher
Thompson (CA)
Thompson (MS)
Towns
Van Hollen
Velázquez
Wasserman Schultz
Waters
Watson
Watt
Welch (VT)
Wexler
Woolsey
Wu
Wynn

**ANSWERED
"PRESENT"—1**
Cohen

NOT VOTING—12
Abercrombie
Davis, Jo Ann
Forbes
Fortuño
Hastert
Hinojosa
LaHood
McNulty
Ortiz
Sessions
Tierney
Waxman

Ms. MOORE of Wisconsin, Mr. MEEHAN, Mr. ALLEN, Ms. BERK-
LEY and Mr. TOWNS changed their vote from "aye" to "no."

Mr. LAMPSON, Mr. HASTINGS of Florida and Ms. JACKSON-LEE of
Texas changed their vote from "no" to "aye."

So the amendment was agreed to.

ABOUT THE AUTHORS

Lynn Woolley

During his Texas-based radio show, Lynn Woolley is the "Secretary of Logic," taking the vital issues of the day, stripping them of their emotion and analyzing them with logic aforethought. Later in the day, he turns from talk show host to political writer, commenting on current events for such venues as the Dallas Morning News and the website **www.HumanEvents.com.** Lynn was recently named to the TALKERS Magazine "Heavy Hundred" as one of the top talk show hosts in America.

Lynn's broadcast career has included stints as a radio news anchor in Dallas and Austin, a political reporter, and a play-by-play announcer. He is the author of three prior books.

He is a past winner of the Dallas Press Club "Katie" award, and has won several Associated Press awards for political commentary. Lynn has been a local TV host of the Children's Miracle Network Telethon in the Waco-Temple market since 1986. He holds a bachelor's degree from the University of Texas at Austin.

His website is **www.BeLogical.com.**

Cliff Kincaid

A veteran journalist and media critic, Cliff Kincaid serves as editor of the Accuracy in Media (AIM) Report and president of America's Survival Inc., a U.N. watchdog group. He concentrated in journalism and communications at the University of Toledo, where he graduated with a Bachelor of Arts degree, and came to Washington through a national journalism program headed by conservative author and journalist M. Stanton Evans. At his college newspaper, Cliff won an award for editorial writing from the Society of Professional Journalists.

Cliff served on the staff of Human Events newspaper for several years and was an editorial writer and newsletter editor for former National Security Council staffer Oliver North at his Freedom Alliance educational foundation. He has written or co-authored nine books on media and cultural affairs and foreign policy issues.

Cliff was a guest co-host on CNN's Crossfire in the 1980s (filling in for Pat Buchanan) and has appeared on numerous television and radio programs. He was a radio talk show host in the 1980s.

AIM's website is **www.aim.org.**

Want more copies of The Death of Talk Radio?

Bulk pricing is available through Accuracy in Media. You can buy a whole box to give out as gifts, donate to libraries or schools, send to your local media or government representatives, or pass out at group meetings.

To order bulk quantities, call us at 1-800-787-4567, order online at ShopAIM.org, send an e-mail to info@aim.org, or write to Accuracy in Media, Attn: Bulk Orders, 4455 Connecticut Ave NW Ste 330, Washington, DC 20008.

For a current catalog of our books, videos and more, contact us at 1-800-787-4567 or info@aim.org.

Please keep in mind that your purchase will benefit Accuracy in Media, a non-profit media watchdog group whose mission is to promote fairness, balance, and accuracy in news reporting.

Additional discounts on AIM's books and other publications are available to members of Accuracy in Media. See the reverse page for details on how to become an AIM member.

Help protect the First Amendment by making a tax-deductible contribution to Accuracy in Media.

Accuracy in Media is a 501(c)(3) non-profit media watchdog group whose mission is to promote fairness, balance, and accuracy in news reporting.

AIM has launched a national campaign to educate the American public about why the Fairness Doctrine is not only unfair, but would actually create a severely unbalanced media. We have been monitoring the political balance of the media since 1969 and have found that the press was far less balanced when it was regulated by the Fairness Doctrine.

We can only carry on this campaign with your help! Please join us today. Your support will make a difference!

Basic memberships start at $40 per year, which includes a subscription to our twice-monthly newsletter, the *AIM Report.* If you donate $50 or more, we will send you a complimentary copy of either *The Death of Talk Radio?* or *Why You Can't Trust the News,* another book we have published about issues with media coverage. You will also be eligible for additional discounts on our books and documentaries.

To make a tax-deductible donation, call 1-800-787-4567, give a secure donation online at www.aim.org, or send a check, money order, or credit card information to Accuracy in Media, 4455 Connecticut Ave NW Ste 330, Washington, DC 20008.